CONTENTS

Introduction 1

Week 1—Trusting God 4

Week 2—Parents 8

Week 3—Purity 12

Week 4—Encouragement 16

Week 5—Discipline 20

Week 6—Acceptance 24

Week 7—Comfort 28

Week 8—Assurance 32

Week 9—Salvation 36

Week 10—Witnessing 40

Week 11—Differences 44

Week 12—Rules 48

Week 13—Scripture Memorization 52

Week 14—Eternal Life 56

Week 15—Hope 60

Week 16—Authority 64

Week 17—God's Faithfulness 68

Week 18—Family 72

Week 19—Boy Decisions 76

Week 20—Loving God 80

Week 21—Loving Others 84

Week 22—Friendship with God 88

Week 23—God's Word 92

Week 24—Compassion 96
Week 25—Patience.. 100
Week 26—Sex.. 104
Week 27—God's Presence... 108
Week 28—Unity 112
Week 29—Prayer.. 116
Week 30—Obedience... 120
Week 31—Life 124
Week 32—Truth 128
Week 33—Marriage.. 132
Week 34—God's Mercy.. 136
Week 35—Victory 140
Week 36—God's Promises 144
Week 37—Dating.. 148
Week 38—Bible Reading 152
Week 39—Self-image.. 156
Week 40—God's Peace... 160
Week 41—Talents and Gifts... 164
Week 42—God's Grace 168
Week 43—Suffering.. 172
Week 44—Quiet Time.. 176
Week 45—Guilt... 180
Week 46—Divorce 184
Week 47—Temptation.. 188
Week 48—Words.. 192
Week 49—Married Love... 196
Week 50—Journaling 200
Week 51—God's Forgiveness.. 204
Week 52—God's Love.. 208
Answers to Fill-in-the-Blank Questions 212
Topical Index.. 217
References 218
About the Authors.. 219

Start Your Day with Point of Grace

Daily Devotional

HOWARD BOOKS
A DIVISION OF SIMON & SCHUSTER
New York   London   Toronto   Sydney

Our purpose at Howard Books is to:

- *Increase faith* in the hearts of growing Christians
- *Inspire holiness* in the lives of believers
- *Instill hope* in the hearts of struggling people everywhere because

He's coming again!

HOWARD
BOOKS

Published by Howard Books, a division of Simon & Schuster, Inc.
1230 Avenue of the Americas, New York, NY 10020
www.howardpublishing.com

Girls of Grace Daily Devotional © 2007 by Point of Grace

Library of Congress Cataloging-in-Publication Data
Girls of grace daily devotional : start your day with Point of Grace.
  p. cm.
  Summary: "Devotional book by Point of Grace provides teen girls with five faith-building activities for each week of the year"—Provided by publisher.
  Includes index.
  1. Teenage girls—Prayers and devotions. I. Point of Grace (Musical group)
  BV4860.G57 2007
  242'.633—dc22

                                                                    2007023298

ISBN-13: 978-1-4165-5396-0
ISBN-10:   1-4165-5396-7

10 9 8 7 6 5 4 3 2 1

Manufactured in the United States of America

For information regarding special discounts for bulk purchases, please contact Simon & Schuster Special Sales at 1-800-456-6798 or business@simonandschuster.com.

Compilation by Snapdragon Group℠ Editorial Services, Tulsa, Oklahoma
Interior Design by Tennille Paden

Opening messages are excerpted and adapted from selected sections of the following books by Point of Grace: *Girls of Grace, Girls of Grace Make It Real, Steady On.*

Our Message to You

How to Use Your Devotional

For as long as we can remember, spending regular time with God has been a top priority for each one of us. It's a little like math (don't worry—it's just a little like math), God "multiplies" (see, there's the math) the small amount of time you spend with Him into big blessings all day long. When you set aside a little quiet time with God—whether it's in the morning, at noon, or at bedtime—your whole day will go so much better and smoother because you have centered yourself on God.

As we've worked on putting this book together, we wished we'd had something like it when we were your age. We just know you're going to love it! It's set up so you have five short and easy devotions for each week of the year. Each week has (1) a brief message, (2) a fill-in-the-blank Bible study, (3) a special scripture for you to read and place in your heart, (4) an action idea for living out that week's message, and (5) some space to journal your thoughts and feelings. The five-devotions-a-week plan allows for a rest on Sunday and a "Yikes! I overslept" day.

One of the cool things about the setup of this devotional is that you can pick and choose which devotion you do on any day of the week—they can be done in any order you choose. Say, on Monday you're in a rush and just have time to read a short scripture. Just go to the "Hear God's Voice" section and read your scripture. But be sure you really read it and let it sink into your heart so you can carry it with you all day long. Then on Tuesday, you might want to do your Bible study; so you back up to the "Get into the Word" section and spend a little more time doing that devotion. Each devotional activity has a flower check box so you can check off each activity as you do it. By the end of the week, you'll have all five flowers checked, and you'll be closer to God, deeper into His Word, and more like Jesus.

We are so proud of you that you have chosen to make God and His Word a part of your daily life. Our hearts are with you each step of the way.

2

Week 1
Trusting God

❀ RESTLESS FEET

We know it's true that we can't see the future like God can, we understand that we don't have the wisdom God has, and it's obvious that we have little power to make good happen. But still, our humanity cries out, "Let me direct my own life!" All the while, God says to us, "Let *me* direct your life. Out of my vision, out of my wisdom, out of my power, out of my compassion and love, let me direct your steps."

Walking steadily beside my God is one of the most terrifying challenges I face in my spiritual life. I have a hard time turning everything over to Him, I struggle with trusting Him to bring people into my life when I need them, and I wrestle with waiting on Him to answer my prayers when I'd rather handle the situation my own way. Even though it's not easy to let go, deep down I know that if I am to have any stability in my life, I *must* let Him lead. I pray, to the depth of my being, that my restless feet will learn to walk beside my loving Father, trusting Him.

GET INTO THE WORD

1. Read Romans 15:13 and fill in the blanks: *May the God of _____ fill you with all _____ and _____ as you _____ in him, so that you may overflow with hope by the _____ of the Holy Spirit.*

2. What benefits of trusting God are revealed in this verse? _____

   _____

   _____

   _____

3. Which of these benefits do you need most in your life right now? Why? _____

   _____

   _____

4. In what ways do you think the Holy Spirit helps you trust God?

   _____

   _____

   _____

   _____

   _____

   _____

🌸 Hear God's Voice

Trust in the LORD with all your heart and lean not on your own understanding; in all your ways acknowledge him, and he will make your paths straight.

—Proverbs 3:5–6

🌸 Live It Out

This week I will step out and trust God by _____

_____

_____

_____

_____

_____

_____

_____

✿ Write It Down

Recall a time when you trusted God and did things His way, even when you were afraid. What did that experience teach you about God? What did it teach you about yourself?

_____

_____

_____

_____

_____

_____

_____

_____

_____

_____

_____

_____

Week 2
Parents

❁ Different Eyes

What does it mean to honor your parents? In the context of Exodus 20:12, "Honor your father and your mother" means to hold them in high esteem and respect. That means being a big enough person to accept what your parents say and obey them whether you agree or not. (Ugh! That's a hard one!)

That's fine until they say no to something you want to do. When I was in seventh grade, my parents wouldn't allow me to go to 8 Wheels—the *only* place for *cool* kids to be on Friday nights. Amazingly, they didn't think a seventh-grade girl should be dropped off by herself at a roller-skating rink where older kids were hanging out and you could come and go as you please. Honestly, looking back, I can see they were right. It was a rather seedy place, but I didn't see it that way then. See? I had different eyes then.

Parents aren't perfect, but no two people love us more or care more about our welfare. They are a big part of God's strategy to keep us safe and happy. When we struggle against them, we are actually struggling against our own best interests. Thank God for your parents. They are one of His greatest gifts to you.

1. Read Hebrews 13:17 and fill in the blanks: *Obey your
    _____ and submit to their authority. They keep watch over
    you as men who must give an _____. Obey them so that their
    _____ will be a joy, not a _____, for that would be of
    no _____ to you.*

2. Do you think of your parents as leaders with authority in your
    life? Why or why not? _____
    _____
    _____

3. In what ways do you think your parents are accountable to God
    for your spiritual, emotional, and physical health and well-being?
    _____
    _____
    _____

4. What are some ways you can thank your parents for all they do on
    your behalf?_____
    _____
    _____
    _____

"Honor your father and mother"—which is the first commandment with a promise—"that it may go well with you and that you may enjoy long life on the earth."

—*Ephesians 6:2–3 NKJV*

LIVE IT OUT

This week I will honor my parents by _____

_____

_____

_____

_____

_____

_____

_____

❋ WRITE IT DOWN

In what specific areas do you find it easy to honor your parents? What is it in you that makes it comfortable for you to submit to their wisdom in those areas? What other areas need work in order for you to give your parents the honor they deserve? Explain why.

_____

_____

_____

_____

_____

_____

_____

_____

_____

_____

_____

❋ NEVER TOO LATE

God has wired us to need intimacy and love, but Satan perverts that need so that we look for it in all the wrong places—and sexual intimacy outside of marriage is one of the places too many girls look.

Maybe you are one of those girls. Or maybe you've never been asked to contemplate how you act on a date. Some kids think that if they abstain from the "technical" act of sex, doing everything else is okay. This way of thinking may keep you from getting pregnant, but it isn't "okay" with God, and the spiritual and psychological damage can be just as severe as "going all the way." Studies show that Christian kids struggle with these issues just as much as non-Christians do.

But it's important to know that it's never too late to make things right—no matter what you've done in the past. Did you know that the word *virgin* actually means "pure"? With God's help, you can be pure in the way you think and the way you act, the way you dress and the way you carry yourself. Your relationship with guys in the future can be all new. You can be a virgin in every sense but the "technical" one.

❁ GET INTO THE WORD

1. Read Psalm 119:9–11(NCV) and fill in the blanks: *How can a young person live a pure life? He can do it by obeying your _____. With all my heart I try to _____ you, God. Don't let me break your _____. I have taken your _____ to heart so I would not _____ against you.*

2. Do you think it was more difficult or less difficult to remain pure in Old Testament times? Why? _____

   _____

   _____

3. What is it about the Word of God that helps you resist temptation? _____

   _____

   _____

4. Why is it important to stay pure in God's eyes, especially in regard to sexual sin? _____

   _____

   _____

   _____

   _____

✿ HEAR GOD'S VOICE

Happy are those who live pure lives, who follow the LORD's teachings.

—*Psalm 119:1 NCV*

✿ LIVE IT OUT

This week I will take a step toward establishing purity in my life by changing the way I _____

_____

_____

_____

_____

_____

_____

❋ WRITE IT DOWN

What do you struggle with most concerning purity (your language, the way you dress, specific behaviors)? What friends and activities do you have that make it easier to maintain purity in your life? What is it about those friends and activities that help you in this area?

_____

_____

_____

_____

_____

_____

_____

_____

_____

_____

_____

Week 4
Encouragement

🌸 GIVE ME A "B"

We all need a cheerleader as we play the game of life, because we all need encouragement from time to time. Life can be hard, and we need someone who can cheer us on and pick us up when we fall down. We need someone who can encourage us when we feel defeated. A cheerleader knows how to find the positive in the negativity of life and invites us to take a new look.

Barnabas, in Acts 9:26–15:39, was the apostle Paul's personal cheerleader. In fact, Barnabas's name means "son of encouragement"! Paul was a formidable persecutor of Christians, costing many of them their lives. When he was converted and became a follower of Christ, the Christians in Jerusalem were afraid of him and wouldn't have anything to do with him. Who could blame them?

Barnabas, however, believed in Paul, took him around to the other believers, and convinced them to take him in. His willingness to stand beside Paul resulted in a long-lasting, trusting relationship between the two men.

I have been blessed to have great encouragers in my life as well. How about you?

❋ GET INTO THE WORD

1. Read Romans 15:4 and fill in the blanks: *Everything that was*

    _____ *in the past was written to* _____ *us, so that*

    through _____ *and the* _____ *of the* _____

    we might have _____.

2. Do you think the apostle Paul said a lot of encouraging things in
    his letters to the early Christians? Why was that so important?

    _____

    _____

    _____

3. There are many encouraging verses in the book of 1 Corinthians.
    Can you find two you really like?_____

    _____

    _____

4. How do you think the verses you've chosen helped the early
    Christians?_____

    _____

    _____

    _____

    _____

✿ Hear God's Voice

Encourage each other and give each other strength, just as you are doing now.

—1 Thessalonians 5:11 NCV

✿ Live It Out

This week I will offer encouragement to _____ by _____

_____

_____

_____

_____

_____

_____

_____

_____

❀ WRITE IT DOWN

Describe a time when someone said something that really made you feel good about yourself. Did that person's words affect the way you behaved and the things you said after that? In what ways? Be specific.

Week 5
Discipline

❀ DAILY TRAINING

"Have you finished your homework?" "Did you clean your room?" "Don't forget to practice the piano." Does any of this sound familiar? Well, it sure does to me, and I remember all too clearly my responses as I huffed and puffed and rolled my eyes on my way to do whatever I was told. However, what I thought was a total pain at the time, I now see was for my own good. It was all a lesson in discipline.

By *discipline,* I don't mean punishment; I mean training or instruction. That's what my parents were trying to do with all their questions and rules: they were training me, teaching me how to live life responsibly.

The definition of *train* is "to form by instruction, discipline, or drill; to teach so as to make fit, qualified, or proficient." In order to have a healthy spiritual life, we must discipline—or train—ourselves daily in Bible reading, prayer, and time with God.

You see, what we don't understand as teenagers—and what our parents already know—is that much of what we learn as young people will establish who we become as adults.

1. Read Hebrews 12:11 and fill in the blanks: *No _____ seems _____ at the time, but painful. Later on, however, it produces a _____ of _____ and _____ for those who have been _____ by it.*

2. What does the word *discipline* mean to you? How is it different from the way it's used in Hebrews 12:11? _____

   _____

   _____

3. In what areas of your life are you being trained? _____

   _____

   _____

4. Read Luke 2:41–52. What does this passage tell you about how Jesus responded to discipline? _____

   _____

   _____

   _____

   _____

   _____

❋ HEAR GOD'S VOICE

Our fathers disciplined us for a little while as they thought best; but God disciplines us for our good, that we may share in his holiness.

—*Hebrews 12:10*

❋ LIVE IT OUT

This week I will choose one area of my life in which I can practice self-discipline by _____

_____

_____

_____

_____

_____

_____

_____

_____

❊ Write It Down

Describe a time when you received a discipline you didn't like, but when it was over, you were totally cool with it and felt it made a positive difference in your life. What obstacles did you have to overcome? What character traits were you trained in during this experience?

Week 6
Acceptance

❋ JUST THE WAY YOU ARE

The need to be loved is one of our strongest emotional longings. When we're feeling bad about ourselves or left out and alone, what we crave is affirmation and acceptance. We usually look to other people for this affirmation and acceptance—kids at school, coworkers, family members, or people at church. And often times, we do get love and acceptance from these people—but not always and not always enough.

On the road, we meet so many girls and guys who feel they don't quite measure up. Maybe they think they're not smart enough, pretty enough, or funny. Whatever they feel is lacking, it's always measured by what other people think and not what God thinks.

I want to tell them, "Who cares if you're not the most popular or if you don't have the so-called coolest clothes? You were designed by Jesus Christ, and, yes, He loves you more than anything—and that's enough." As God's children, we can hold our heads up high, knowing that our identity comes from God. He created us just the way we are—on purpose—and he has a plan for our lives.

GET INTO THE WORD

1. Read Ephesians 1:3–6 and fill in the blanks: *Praise be to the God and Father of our Lord Jesus Christ, who has _____ us in the heavenly realms with every spiritual _____ in Christ. For he chose us in him before the _____ of the _____ to be holy and _____ in his sight. In love he predestined us to be _____ as his sons through Jesus Christ, in accordance with his _____ and _____.*

2. Does God accept everyone, or just those who are really good?

   _____

   _____

3. Is it possible to be good enough for God to call you His child? How does Jesus make you *more* than good enough? _____

   _____

   _____

   _____

4. Why is God's opinion about you the only one that really counts?

   _____

   _____

   _____

❋ HEAR GOD'S VOICE

Accept one another, then, just as Christ accepted you,
in order to bring praise to God.

—*Romans 15:7*

❋ LIVE IT OUT

This week I will reach out to someone who I know is struggling with acceptance and encourage that person by _____

_____

_____

_____

_____

_____

_____

_____

❀ WRITE IT DOWN

Describe a situation when you felt really accepted by someone or by a group. How did it make you feel? What does it mean to you to know that God accepts you just as you are? What are some ways you can pass that on to others?

_____

_____

_____

_____

_____

_____

_____

_____

_____

_____

_____

_____

_____

Week 7
Comfort

❀ SOMETIMES IT HURTS

After leaving the studio one day, I pulled into the driveway, and my husband, Stu, met me outside. Our dog, Freethrow, had been hit by a car. With sadness in his voice, Stu told me that he had died on the way to the veterinarian. We cried together for at least an hour. I know losing a dog is a minor thing compared to the terrible pain some people must endure. Still, I was really hurting. We'd lost our sweet puppy!

In life, everything can be going along exactly as we want it to, and *wham!* All of a sudden something happens, and we are hurting. In some cases, the pain is so bad that we don't want to get up in the morning because we just don't think we can face the day. And it seems that surely no one can understand how we feel.

You, my friend, may be hurting today. If you will let go and let God reach into your heart and open your eyes, you will see—like I did—that He is right beside you, and His big, strong arms are wrapped securely around you. You can know that He will never leave you, that He will never let you down. Allow Him to comfort you.

❀ GET INTO THE WORD

1. Read 2 Corinthians 1:3–4 and fill in the blanks: *Praise be to the God and Father of our Lord Jesus Christ, the Father of _____ and the God of all _____, who comforts us in all our _____, so that we can comfort those in any trouble with the _____ we ourselves have received from God.*

2. How do painful experiences help us to focus on and trust in God's love? _____

   _____

   _____

3. When you think of the pain God suffered when He watched His own Son die, how does that give you strength to endure your present heartache? _____

   _____

   _____

4. God says He comforts us, and then He asks us to do what? _____

   _____

   _____

   _____

   _____

❋ HEAR GOD'S VOICE

The LORD will hear your crying, and he will comfort you. When he hears you, he will help you.

—*Isaiah 30:19 NCV*

❋ LIVE IT OUT

This week I will reach out to someone who is hurting by _____:

_____

_____

_____

_____

_____

_____

_____

_____

WRITE IT DOWN

Describe a specific situation in your life when you needed comfort. Were you able to lean on God's love at that time? Did God use a certain person to minister His love to you? What did you learn from the experience, and how can you use it to comfort those around you who are hurting?

_____

_____

_____

_____

_____

_____

_____

_____

_____

_____

_____

_____

Week 8
Assurance

❀ No Matter What!

I blow it daily, and daily I need to be assured of God's grace. I need to be reminded that He loves me—*no matter what*! Think about the no-matter-whats in your life. You know what I'm talking about. The words you said. The lie you told. The thing you did. The secret you are holding inside. You need someone in your life who will assure you that the grace of God is with you no matter what. And you need to be the kind of person who assures other people in the same way.

In 1 Peter, Peter was writing to believers who were undergoing severe persecution, assuring them that "no matter what" happened to them, they were not alone. God was with them, and His grace surrounded them. So no matter what happens to you, God is right beside you. He doesn't always take the pain away, but He cries with you.

Are you the kind of friend who encourages others to look to God's grace when the no-matter-whats of life start pressing in? Do you have friends who help you do the same? If you don't have friends like that, the choice is up to you. Remember, be that kind of friend, and you will attract that kind of friend.

❈ GET INTO THE WORD

1. Read Romans 8:38–39 and fill in the blanks: *I am convinced that neither _____ nor _____, neither _____ nor _____, neither the _____ nor the _____, nor any _____, neither _____ nor _____, nor anything else in all creation, will be able to separate us from the love of God that is in Christ Jesus our Lord.*

2. Can you think of anything you might encounter in your life that isn't covered by this verse? _____
    _____
    _____

3. Why do you think God is willing to give us this blanket assurance, even though we often fail Him? _____
    _____
    _____

4. Is it possible for anyone but God to make this kind of promise? Why? _____
    _____
    _____
    _____

My purpose in writing is to encourage you and assure you that the grace of God is with you no matter what happens.

—*1 Peter 5:12* NLT

🌸 LIVE IT OUT

This week I will choose one area where I feel secure in my relationship with God and share it with a friend who is struggling in that area by

_____

_____

_____

_____

_____

_____

_____

❀ Write It Down

Describe a situation when you felt God was really there for you. How did that make you feel? Can you think of other situations where you weren't as aware that God was with you, but you see now that He was? As you think back, what little things, which you might have overlooked at the time, are more obvious now?

Salvation

🌸 REFLECTING GOD'S IMAGE

God is *invisible*. We can't see Him, so how can we reflect His image? That's where Jesus comes in. Jesus showed us in living color—in flesh and blood—what God looked like. So if we want to know what God *really* looks like, all we have to do is look at Jesus, the fairest of them all.

When we repent of our sins and trust Jesus as our Savior, we are completely renewed—becoming like Him, reflecting God's image! Before our renewal we used our God-imaging powers in wrong ways, but now we are enabled to use these powers in right ways.

God's purpose in creating you and me in His image was fulfilled in Jesus Christ. So as we trust in Him, we can be assured that our sins are forgiven, and our purpose and mission in being God's image bearers are restored. In fact, it could be said that the goal of our salvation in Christ is to make us more and more like God, or more and more like Christ, who is the perfect image of God (see Romans 8:29). That is what sets us apart from all of God's creatures. And as we become more and more like God, the story of our image becomes clearer as we reflect our Creator.

GET INTO THE WORD

1. Read Titus 3:4–5 and fill in the blanks: *When the _____ and love of God our Savior appeared, he _____ us, not because of _____ things we had done, but because of his _____. He saved us through the _____ of rebirth and _____ by the Holy Spirit.*

2. What is it we are being saved from? Provide at least five answers.

   _____

   _____

   _____

   _____

   _____

3. What is it we are being saved to? Provide at least five answers.

   _____

   _____

   _____

   _____

   _____

4. Is there something we must do in response to God's grace? What is it? _____

   _____

❀ HEAR GOD'S VOICE

You have taken off your old self with its practices and have put on the new self, which is being renewed in knowledge in the image of its Creator.

—*Colossians 3:9–10*

❀ LIVE IT OUT

This week I will step out to become more like God in one particular aspect of my life by _____

_____

_____

_____

_____

_____

_____

🌸 WRITE IT DOWN

In what areas of your life do you feel you already do a good job of reflecting God's image? What areas could use improvement? Jot down some ideas for working on your most challenging area. _____

_____

_____

_____

_____

_____

_____

_____

_____

_____

_____

Week 10
Witnessing

❀ SANCTIFIED GOSSIP

The very first people who heard the greatest news that ever was or ever will be received by humankind—that Jesus Christ had risen from the dead—were three women. Not three men. Three women. Then just a couple of verses down, Jesus Himself first appeared after his triumph over death to Mary Magdalene, a woman who began to spread what Beth Moore so suitably calls "the first ever recorded case of sanctified gossip"!

My friends, it was not an accident that Jesus chose women first to get the word out. He knew we could do it! I believe it was completely by design. Telling the good news of Christ is by far the very best thing we can be spreading around. In fact, we are commanded to use our mouths to tell others about the awesome and noncondemning love of God.

People in this day and age really need to hear this news! The world we live in is so depressing sometimes that we can't even think straight. Using our mouths to witness and show God's love to others would be using them exactly the way they were meant to be used.

✿ Get into the Word

1. Read Matthew 5:14–16 and fill in the blanks: *You are the _____ of the world. A city on a hill cannot be _____. Neither do people light a _____ and put it under a bowl. Instead they put it on its _____, and it gives light to everyone in the house. In the same way, let your _____ shine before _____, that they may see your _____ deeds and _____ your Father in heaven.*

2. Why is it so important to tell others about your faith? _____
   _____
   _____

3. Name two ways sharing your faith with others helps *you*. _____
   _____
   _____

   Name two ways sharing your faith with others helps *others*. _____
   _____
   _____

4. Does God suggest that we witness to others, or does He command us to do so? Explain your answer._____
   _____
   _____

🌸 HEAR GOD'S VOICE

We saw it, we heard it, and now we're telling you so you can experience it along with us, this experience of communion with the Father and his Son, Jesus Christ.

—*1 John 1:3* MSG

🌸 LIVE IT OUT

This week I will share my faith with someone either in word or deed by

_____

_____

_____

_____

_____

_____

_____

_____

❈ WRITE IT DOWN

How does it make you feel to share your faith with another person? List three primary emotions you experience. Why do you think God asks you to witness to others when He could tell them Himself? Jot down some witnessing strategies that should work in your life now.

_____

_____

_____

_____

_____

_____

_____

_____

_____

_____

_____

Week 11
Differences

❀ COMPLETELY UNIQUE

It amazes me every day how different the four of us in Point of Grace are. Just taking a look at each of our closets will show you some of our differences. For instance, if you were to look in Shelley's or Leigh's closets, you would find them to be very neat, tidy, and organized. Mine and Heather's would look quite different. *Messy* would be Shelley's choice word for our closets. Mine might look a little more organized than Heather's, but let's just say that organization isn't either of our strengths.

Just as our closets are different, so are our personalities. I'm hyper, bouncy, competitive, and always want to be on the go. Heather is laid-back, a deep thinker, and takes things in stride. Shelley is in control and a great leader. She always knows how to motivate the rest of us. Leigh is the encourager, always wanting to help out where she is needed. I love how God chose to make us all unique.

You were uniquely made as well. Celebrate the fact that you are different from anyone else you know. It proves you were crafted by a brilliant and creative God.

GET INTO THE WORD

1. Read Romans 12:4–6 and fill in the blanks: *Just as each of us has one* _____ *with many* _____, *and these members do not all have the same* _____, *so in Christ we who are many form one* _____, *and each member belongs to all the* _____. *We have different* _____, *according to the* _____ *given us.*

2. What do you think this verse teaches us about the importance of our differences? _____

   _____

   _____

2. What personality trait or gift do you see in your three best friends that you don't see in yourself? _____

   _____

   _____

4. What personality trait or gift do you see in yourself that is not obvious in your three best friends? _____

   _____

   _____

   _____

   _____

❀ Hear God's Voice

You created my inmost being;
you knit me together in my mother's womb.
I praise you because I am fearfully and wonderfully made;
your works are wonderful, I know that full well.

—Psalm 139:13–14

❀ Live It Out

This week I will celebrate the differences between me and another person
by _____

_____

_____

_____

_____

_____

_____

❋ Write It Down

How does it make you feel to know your friends are strong in some areas where you are not? What are some ways their unique personality traits and gifts can bless your life? Explain how. What unique personality traits and gifts do you have that can bless their lives? Explain how.

_____

_____

_____

_____

_____

_____

_____

_____

_____

_____

Week 12
Rules

✿ For Your Own Good

When I was a teenager, I asked my mom if I could go to a party at my friend's house. Mom responded quickly with a firm "No!" I pleaded and gave her every reason in the book why I should be allowed to go. "You're not being fair," I pouted. Her final response was, "I'm concerned that some things may be going on at that party you should not be involved in." Shamefully, I confess that I found a way and went to the party, only to learn that she was absolutely correct in her assumptions.

Why do we have such a hard time accepting rules that are for our own good? It may have something to do with the fact that we live in a fallen world; and where humanity is, there is sin. This is not an excuse to give up the fight. However, it reiterates the importance of having godly people in our lives to hold us accountable for the choices we make.

In reality, it's hard to force other people to do things they don't want to do. But a good authority figure does enforce the rules by imposing consequences when the rules are broken. And sometimes life imposes those consequences naturally.

1. Read Psalm 119:156 and fill in the blanks: *Your _____ is great, O LORD; _____ my _____ according to your _____.*

2. What do you think this verse teaches is the primary reason for God's laws? Explain your answer. _____

    _____

    _____

    _____

    _____

    _____

3. How can the Bible say we are free when God expects us to obey His laws (rules) and our parents' rules? _____

    _____

    _____

    _____

    _____

    _____

❊ Hear God's Voice

How blessed the man you train, God,
the woman you instruct in your Word,
Providing a circle of quiet within the clamor of evil.

—*Psalm 94:12–13* MSG

❊ Live It Out

This week I will take a step toward amending my attitude about rules by

1. Obeying my parents the first time they ask me to do something.

2. Making the choice not to question their judgment about a certain rule.

3. _____

    _____

    _____

    _____

    _____

❋ WRITE IT DOWN

Why do you think *rules* sometimes rub us the wrong way? What do you think the world would be like without rules? What rules can you easily see are designed to protect you? What rules do you have trouble accepting? What are some ways you can change your attitude about those rules?

_____

_____

_____

_____

_____

_____

_____

_____

_____

_____

_____

Week 13
Scripture Memorization

❀ SEIZE THE POWER

A truly vital spiritual discipline is memorizing scripture. Doing this will help you grow in intimacy with God and will help you be more effective in living out His will for your life.

Let me share some tactics that have helped me in this discipline:

- Write the verses you are memorizing on sticky notes and place them where you will see them during the day.

- Write your memory verses in your journal.

- Find a friend who will memorize along with you, and offer each other incentives—the last one to memorize a certain scripture has to treat the other to a meal.

- Say the verses in your mind right before you go to sleep.

It's amazing how the passages of Scripture I commit to memory pop up in my mind just when I need them. Whether I am being tempted or am presented with a ministry opportunity, God's words are much more powerful than my own.

🌸 GET INTO THE WORD

1. Read Jeremiah 15:16 and fill in the blanks: *When your _____ came, I ate them; they were my _____ and my heart's _____, for I _____ your name, O LORD God Almighty.*

2. When Jeremiah says he *ate* God's words, what do you think he meant? _____

   _____

   _____

3. In what practical ways can having God's words on the tip of your tongue help you be a stronger Christian? _____

   _____

   _____

4. Why was it important for early Christians to memorize scripture?

   _____

   _____

   _____

   _____

   _____

   _____

❋ HEAR GOD'S VOICE

I have hidden your word in my heart
that I might not sin against you.

—Psalm 119:11

❋ LIVE IT OUT

This week I will write out _____, carry it with me, and read it whenever I'm alone, until I can say the whole verse by memory. (If you don't already have a favorite, try John 3:16, 1 John 1:9, or Romans 12:1–2.)

_____

_____

_____

_____

_____

_____

❋ WRITE IT DOWN

How would you feel if you were no longer permitted to read the Bible? How would that change the way you feel about being a Christian? What verse would you want to memorize so you would always have it with you? Describe what that verse means to you.

Week 14
Eternal Life

PAPA AND JESUS

On the last day of his life, as I sat with my grandpa, holding his hand, my heart was heavy and burdened. He said nothing, but for one brief moment he squeezed my hand to acknowledge my presence. A few hours later, he passed away.

During the next few days, I worried and wondered where my grandfather was spending eternity. I felt guilty and selfish and stupid that I had not been able to swallow my pride and talked with Papa about Jesus while he was still alive. I came up with a million reasons why I hadn't, but not a single one was reason enough—not when it had been a matter of eternal life and death. But on the day of the funeral, the preacher told us that a few weeks before his death, he and Papa had prayed together, and Papa had accepted Christ. After the service, I found the preacher in the parking lot and hugged his neck. "Thank you for telling Papa about Jesus!" I'm still thankful to him today.

Is there someone in your life you need to share Christ with? I urge you not to be like me and leave it to someone else. Don't wait—open your mouth and share the Good News about Jesus.

🌸 Get into the Word

1. Read John 11:25–26 and fill in the blanks: *Jesus said to her, "I am the _____ and the _____. He who _____ in me will live, even though he _____; and whoever _____ and believes in me will _____ die. Do you believe this?"*

2. When the Bible says "believes in me," what does it mean? Does it simply mean believing that Jesus was a real person, or does it mean more? _____

_____

_____

3. How long is eternal life? When does your eternal life start? When does it end? _____

_____

_____

4. What do you think will be the best part about living eternally with God? _____

_____

_____

_____

_____

🌸 HEAR GOD'S VOICE

Jesus said, "Everyone who believes can have eternal life in him. God loved the world so much that he gave his one and only Son so that whoever believes in him may not be lost, but have eternal life."

—*John 3:16 NCV*

🌸 LIVE IT OUT

This week I will tell someone about the gift of eternal life and how God has promised it to everyone who _____

_____

_____

_____

_____

_____

_____

❀ WRITE IT DOWN

What do you think it will be like when you see Jesus for the first time?
How will you express your love for Him? How does it make you feel
when you think about living in God's presence forever? Describe how
you imagine it will be.

_____

_____

_____

_____

_____

_____

_____

_____

_____

_____

_____

_____

Week 15
Hope

❁ HOPE AND A FUTURE

Life is hard, isn't it? We all have had our share of disappointment, pain, and grief. The hopeless state of our world is plain to see, and it's depressing to see all the pain and destruction around us. Some things we bring on ourselves, but others, such as tornadoes, floods, or car accidents, are completely outside our control.

Some of you reading this are going through intense pain right now. Perhaps you've lost someone you love. Maybe your relationship with your most important person in the world is falling apart. Maybe your health or physical disabilities keep you from living life as you'd like. My heart is heavy for those of you who hurt.

But I don't really want to talk about suffering. What I want to talk about is hope. One definition of *hope* is "to anticipate with pleasure; waiting with expectancy." In the New Testament, hope centers on Jesus Christ Himself. He is our hope. What do you hope for?

Hope and a future! Isn't that what we all want? God has plans for us—plans to prosper us. Isn't that wonderful? How blessed we are!

🌸 GET INTO THE WORD

1. Read Jeremiah 29:11 and fill in the blanks: *"I know the _____ I have for you," declares the LORD, "plans to _____ you and not to _____ you, plans to give you _____ and a _____."*

2. Do you know what God's plan is for your future? How do you think you can find out? _____

   _____

   _____

3. How do you know God's plan for you will succeed regardless of your present circumstances? _____

   _____

   _____

   _____

4. Who is responsible for seeing that God's plan comes to pass in your life—you or God? Explain. _____

   _____

   _____

   _____

   _____

   _____

✿ HEAR GOD'S VOICE

Those who hope in the LORD
will renew their strength.
They will soar on wings like eagles;
they will run and not grow weary,
they will walk and not be faint.

—*Isaiah 40:31*

✿ LIVE IT OUT

This week I will begin to seek out God's plan for my life by praying with and consulting the wisdom of these adults in my life:

1. _____

2. _____

❀ WRITE IT DOWN

Describe the plan you would choose for your life. How do you think it would compare to the plan God has for you? How do you think they would be similar? How do you think they would be different?

_____

_____

_____

_____

_____

_____

_____

_____

_____

_____

_____

_____

_____

_____

Authority

❀ WHO'S IN CHARGE HERE?

Unfortunately, we live in a world where not everyone who sets himself up as an authority figure can be trusted. If someone in authority is forcing things on you that you know are wrong, get help from an adult. If the first adult you talk to doesn't help you, keep going until you find someone who will.

With that said, there are many wonderful people in your life who—though not perfect—are to be trusted and followed. These people bring wisdom, enforce rules, and provide protective boundaries. They are looking out for your good, and they are worthy of your respect.

For example, when your parents say you can't go to a particular party, they aren't trying to spoil your fun; they are doing it for your own good. This is where trust comes in. If your youth pastor sets up boundaries for a trip the youth group is taking, out of respect and trust, you stay within those boundaries—partly because it's right to obey his authority, and partly because you trust his judgment.

Of course, Jesus Christ is the ultimate authority in our lives. We can always trust His judgments.

❀ GET INTO THE WORD

1. Read Romans 13:1 and fill in the blanks: *Everyone must _____ himself to the governing authorities, for there is no _____ except that which God has established. The authorities that exist have been established by _____.*

2. What should you do if an authority figure in your life asks you to do something that would not be pleasing to God? How should you handle that if it happens? _____

    _____

    _____

3. What are the benefits of honoring the authority God has placed in your life? _____

    _____

    _____

    _____

4. Who will those in authority answer to? Why is that important?

    _____

    _____

    _____

    _____

❀ Hear God's Voice

Obey your parents in everything, for this pleases the Lord.

—*Colossians 3:20*

❀ Live It Out

This week I will personally thank two authority figures in my life for taking the responsibility of helping me become the person God created me to be. The two I want to thank are:

1. _____

2. _____

✤ WRITE IT DOWN

When you are in a position of authority as an adult, what principles will guide how you treat those God has placed in your care? Reflecting on how the authority figures in your life relate to you, what will you do differently? What will you do the same? Be specific.

_____

_____

_____

_____

_____

_____

_____

_____

_____

_____

_____

_____

Week 17
God's Faithfulness

✿ THE NARROW ROAD

Have you ever taken a detour on the journey of life, strayed from the narrow road, and lost your way? We've all been there. We've all strayed. It's easy to get distracted and turn from the path God has laid out for us.

I've taken many wrong turns and a few detours, and I've lost my way in the wilderness countless times. But somehow I always find my way back to the road, the narrow road. My Master keeps it all lit up for me, so I'll always be able to find my way home.

You know how on hot summer nights, you can see the lights of a softball field all the way across town? If you follow the lights, you can find your way to the field. God's light is like that. It penetrates the darkness and shines steadfastly. If you keep making your way toward it, you'll eventually end up right there with Him.

Because I carry the name of Christ, I am called to live by a higher standard. I will never be like Him completely, but I will strive to be more like Him every day. And if I stray, He faithfully waits for me at the end of the well-lit road.

❀ GET INTO THE WORD

1. Read Psalm 119:105 and fill in the blanks: *Your* _____ *is a*
    _____ *to my feet and a* _____ *for my* _____.

2. Why is God's Word so important when it comes to walking on the
    narrow road and staying free from sin?_____
    _____
    _____
    _____

3. Name three things that indicate the faithfulness of God in your
    daily life. _____
    _____
    _____
    _____

4. In what ways can God's faithfulness make you more faithful to
    those you love?_____
    _____
    _____
    _____
    _____
    _____

❁ HEAR GOD'S VOICE

If we confess our sins, he is faithful and just and will forgive us our sins and purify us from all unrighteousness.

—1 John 1:9

❁ LIVE IT OUT

This week I will practice the presence of God by imagining that He is with me at all times, going where I go, hearing all that I say, and seeing everything I do. (In reality, He is and does!) In this way, I will begin to be consciously aware of His faithfulness to me at all times._____

_____

_____

_____

_____

_____

❋ WRITE IT DOWN

Describe how you feel knowing that God is always with you. How does it feel to know that God faithfully forgives every sin—no matter how big or small? Write down your words of praise for His faithfulness.

_____

_____

_____

_____

_____

_____

_____

_____

_____

_____

_____

_____

_____

Family

❀ My Sister, My Sister

Why is it that we fight with our siblings like there's no tomorrow, but we're so utterly concerned about getting along with our friends? I remember walking on eggshells to avoid confrontation with my friends because I was so obsessed with wanting them to like me. But I never had a second thought about going off on my sister.

I've tried to understand why I treated her so badly, and I think I have the answer. Unlike people unrelated to me (like my friends), she couldn't disown me or walk away from me for good. After all, she was my sister—my own flesh and blood—so I felt I could treat her any way I wanted. It just seemed like no big deal. She happened to be the closest, easiest "scapegoat."

But you see, the very thing I thought justified my treating her so badly is the very thing that should have made me treat her with the utmost love and respect. Because she is my flesh and blood, she is one of the few people who will actually remain with me throughout my life, one of the people I can completely trust. She—above all other friends—deserved my highest esteem. How about your sisters and brothers?

❋ GET INTO THE WORD

1. Read Romans 12:10 and fill in the blanks: *Be _____ to one another in _____ love. _____ one another above _____.*

2. In the verse above, is the writer talking about your earthly family, your spiritual family (other Christians), or both? Explain. _____

    _____

    _____

    _____

3. Why is it so important to God that you honor your sisters and brothers? _____

    _____

    _____

    _____

4. Name three benefits of treating your family members with honor and esteem. _____

    _____

    _____

    _____

    _____

✿ HEAR GOD'S VOICE

It is truly wonderful
when relatives live together
in peace.

Psalm 133:1 CEV

✿ LIVE IT OUT

This week I will show honor for my brothers and sisters by _____

_____

_____

_____

_____

_____

_____

_____

🌸 WRITE IT DOWN

Describe each member of your family and write down what that person means to you. Name some of the things that person has done for you. Note specific examples. Write a little prayer of thanks to God for each person.

_____

_____

_____

_____

_____

_____

_____

_____

_____

_____

_____

_____

Week 19
Boy Decisions

❋ HOW FAR IS TOO FAR?

What's the first thing you should do if there's a particular guy you want to get to know better? When I was a teen, the first thing I did was try to be around the guy and flirt to make him notice me. Not too smart. These guidelines have helped me:

Pray about it. Tell God how you feel about the guy. He'll help you see things clearly.

Check your motives. Do I want to date this guy to make myself look good? Do I just want *someone* to date so I'll fit in with everyone else?

If he asks you out, stop and pray about it again. After you climb off the ceiling and call your girlfriends, you really need to pray again.

Set boundaries and plan ahead. If it seems right, say "Yes," but proceed with caution. You can't wait until you're with a guy in a parked car to make good choices.

Know how far is too far. When you ask this question, make sure you're not just wanting to know how much you can get away with. Remember, even kissing can be too intimate in some relationships. Allow the Holy Spirit to speak to you long before your date.

76

❋ GET INTO THE WORD

1. Read 1 Samuel 16:7 and fill in the blanks: *The LORD does not _____ at the things man looks at. _____ looks at the outward _____, but the _____ looks at the _____.*

2. What does the scripture above mean when it says God looks at a person's heart? _____

   _____

   _____

   _____

   _____

3. Why is it dangerous to rely completely on first impressions and physical attraction? _____

   _____

   _____

   _____

   _____

   _____

   _____

🌸 Hear God's Voice

[Don't just grab] whatever attracts your fancy. That's a life shaped by things and feelings instead of by God.

—Colossians 3:5 MSG

🌸 Live It Out

This week I will practice being wise in my relationships, especially with guys, by _____

_____

_____

_____

_____

_____

_____

❀ WRITE IT DOWN

Describe how you feel when you meet someone you feel an attraction to. How do you typically respond to that attraction? What would be the benefits of asking God to help you see past the surface things and focus on the goodness of a person's heart?

_____

_____

_____

_____

_____

_____

_____

_____

_____

_____

Loving God

🌸 When You Love Someone

The fact of the matter is that we all desperately need God. He is the life-giver and the One who nurtures our souls and lavishes His amazing love on us each day. When we go about our day without making Him part of it, we are inadvertently saying to Him that we don't need Him.

Once, when Jesus was asked which of the commandments was the greatest, He quickly replied: "You shall love the Lord your God with all your heart and with all your soul, and with all your mind. This is the great and foremost commandment" (Matthew 22:37–38 NASB). Do you love Him like that? If not, wouldn't you like to? You can if you get in the Word. When you love someone, you desire to spend time with him or her. Do you long to spend time with God? When was the last time you read His Word and prayed to Him?

My friend, God delights in you—He has already given you His amazing, unconditional love—and His plan is for you to delight in Him by loving Him in return.

❧ GET INTO THE WORD

1. Read John 14:21 and fill in the blanks: *Jesus said, "Whoever has my _____ and obeys them, he is the one who _____ me. He who loves me will be _____ by my _____, and I too will love him and _____ myself to him."*

2. Why does God say you don't love Him if you don't obey Him?

   _____

   _____

   _____

   _____

   _____

3. Did Jesus show His love for His Father by obeying Him? Explain your answer._____

   _____

   _____

   _____

   _____

   _____

   _____

✿ Hear God's Voice

Love the LORD your God, listen to his voice, and hold fast to him. For the LORD is your life.

—*Deuteronomy 30:20*

✿ Live It Out

This week I will choose to show my love for God by obeying Him in an area of my life in which I have previously resisted by _____

_____

_____

_____

_____

_____

_____

❋ WRITE IT DOWN

Describe your love for God. Make a list of the things He has brought to your life that would otherwise be missing. Write Him a little prayer of thanksgiving for each one.

Week 21
Loving Others

❀ WHAT DOES LOVE LOOK LIKE?

As a teenager, I used to listen to a Christian band called Whiteheart. One of its songs has always stuck with me. The chorus said, "Let your first thought, let your very first thought be love." Can you imagine how pleased God would be if we could train our hearts and mouths to employ that principle?

When someone has done something to make you mad, let your first thought be love. Now, I'll be the first to admit that this kind of response is not easy, but it is so much better than the alternative. Ask yourself: What does love look like in this situation? A soft, sweet reply? Turning the other cheek? Maybe just listening instead of turning away? Proverbs 15:1 reminds us that "a gentle answer turns away wrath, but a harsh word stirs up anger" (NIV).

When you are having a problem with someone, say a quick prayer: "Jesus, help my first thought to be love." Just try it. Train yourself to take time to think and pray before you react. You won't always remember (I know, I've tried it on my husband!), but eventually God will bless your obedience, and a response of love might even become automatic and truly authentic.

❀ Get into the Word

1. Read 1 Corinthians 13:4–8 and fill in the blanks: *Love is _____, love is kind. It does not _____, it is not proud. It is not _____, it is not self-seeking, it is not easily _____, it keeps no record of _____. Love does not delight in _____ but rejoices with the _____. It always protects, always _____, always hopes, always _____. Love never _____.*

2. How does God's description of love differ from what the world says about it? _____
   _____
   _____

3. If we love others according to God's standard, will they love us in the same way? Why do you think so? _____
   _____
   _____

4. Does loving someone mean that we must indulge them when they behave badly? How should we respond in such a situation? _____
   _____
   _____
   _____

❋ Hear God's Voice

Live a life filled with love, following the example of Christ.

—*Ephesians 5:2* NLT

❋ Live It Out

This week I will practice God's kind of love toward someone I struggle with by _____

_____

_____

_____

_____

_____

_____

_____

✳ Write It Down

Why do you think it is so important to God that we love one another? Do you think loving someone the way God asks you to will change the other person? Do you think it will change you? In what ways? Explain your answer.

_____

_____

_____

_____

_____

_____

_____

_____

_____

_____

_____

Week 22
Friendship with God

❀ Nothing Fickle about Him

Have you ever felt fickle toward God? Do you know what I mean? Some days, I think He's the greatest thing in my life, and I don't know what I would do without Him. Other days—especially when it's been a while since I've had some quality time with Him—I can't feel much of a spark. As much as three weeks can pass before I realize how long it's been since I've spoken to Him. But the amazing thing about God is that even when I lag behind in our relationship, He never lets me go.

The other day, I was telling my dear friend Rose Ann how busy I'd been and how guilty I felt because I hadn't even opened my Bible for a week. I was feeling distant from God. The longer I stayed away, the more awkward I felt. You know how you feel when you haven't called a friend in a long time? When you finally think about calling, you feel weird about it.

Rose Ann reminded me that God is a faithful Friend and Father. Even when we don't hold up our end of the relationship, He remains constant. He loves us. He has so much to share with us that He can't wait for us to pick up the phone and call.

❋ GET INTO THE WORD

1. Read John 15:13–14 and fill in the blanks: *[Jesus said]: "Greater _____ has no one than this, that he lay down his _____ for his _____. You are my friends if you _____ what I _____."*

2. When Jesus said to obey His command in the verse above, which command was He talking about? Look at John 15:9–11. _____

   _____

   _____

   _____

3. What does this tell us about the basic nature of friendship? _____

   _____

   _____

   _____

4. What is the second most important characteristic of friendship? It follows the first. _____

   _____

   _____

   _____

   _____

❀ HEAR GOD'S VOICE

[Jesus said]: "I no longer call you servants ... now you are my friends."

—John 15:15 NLT

❀ LIVE IT OUT

This week I will ask God, my best friend, to help me be a better friend to others by _____

_____

_____

_____

_____

_____

_____

❋ Write It Down

Describe how it makes you feel, just knowing that God wants to be your friend. List the characteristics you feel are most important in a "best" friend. How does God measure up to each one? Write Him a little prayer of thanks for His friendship.

God's Word

❊ THE B-I-B-L-E

One of the first songs I ever learned was "The B-i-b-l-e." Remember that song? "The B-i-b-l-e, yes, that's the book for me. I stand alone on the Word of God, the B-i-b-l-e." I love that song.

I'll never forget the day I got my first Bible. It was white and had beautifully colored pictures in it. I felt very grown up when I carried it to church for the first time. I grew up knowing that the Bible was God's Word, and that it was a very important book. Now that I am older, I see that reading the Bible is not just important—it is vital to the Christian walk.

The Bible is God's thoughts to us. I like that idea. In addition to giving us insight into how God thinks, the Bible is the primary way that God speaks to us. His Word teaches us how to live a life that pleases Him and glorifies His name. The way we get to know Jesus better is by reading and studying the Bible.

My friend, reading God's Word is one of the most important parts of becoming a godly young woman. I pray that you will make them a consistent part of your life. I promise that, if you do, you will be richly rewarded.

❀ GET INTO THE WORD

1. Read Hebrews 4:12 and fill in the blanks: *The Word of God is
   _____ and active. Sharper than any _____ sword, it
   penetrates even to dividing soul and spirit, joints and marrow; it
   _____ the thoughts and _____ of the _____.*

2. Why do you think the Bible is called "God's Word"? _____
   _____
   _____
   _____

3. The verse above says that the Bible is living and active. What do
   you think that means? _____
   _____
   _____
   _____

4. Through prayer, we talk to God; through the Bible, _____
   talks to _____. Explain what this means. _____
   _____
   _____
   _____
   _____

❋ HEAR GOD'S VOICE

God has breathed life into all of Scripture. It is useful for teaching us what is true ... for correcting our mistakes ... for making our lives whole again ... for training us to do what is right. By using Scripture, a man of God can be completely prepared to do every good thing.

—2 Timothy 3:16–17 NIrV

❋ LIVE IT OUT

This week I will find two encouraging verses from the Bible and write them out. Then I will share them with a friend when she seems down. (Suggestions: Romans 8:31 and Jeremiah 29:12–13.)

_____

_____

_____

_____

_____

_____

❀ WRITE IT DOWN

Describe a time when you read a verse of the Bible and it changed your mind about something or changed your attitude in general. Note some other thoughts and attitudes you believe could be changed by reading the Word of God. Make a list.

_____

_____

_____

_____

_____

_____

_____

_____

_____

_____

_____

Week 24
Compassion

✿ A Special Place in His Heart

The Bible says that God is a "father to the fatherless" and a "defender of widows" (see Psalm 68:5–6 NLT). Isn't this a beautiful picture of a loving God? It goes on to say that He "places the lonely in families" and "sets the prisoners free and gives them joy." When we feel lonely, isn't that what we want—to be part of a family, to belong? And have you ever felt like a prisoner in your home circumstances?

There are many other places in the Bible that talk about God's special love for the fatherless: Deuteronomy 10:18 says, "He defends the cause of the fatherless and the widow," and Psalm 27:10 says, "Even if my father and mother abandon me, the Lord will hold me close" (NLT).

Do you get the feeling that God has a special place in His heart for those who are without a father or mother? Can't you hear His compassion and protection ringing loudly from those scriptures?

I've always thought that God has something extra-special in mind for those who grow up without an earthly father or mother. Following His example, shouldn't we be showing compassion to them as well?

❋ GET INTO THE WORD

1. Read Psalm 103:13 and fill in the blanks: *As a father has* _____ *on his* _____, *so the LORD has* _____ *on those who* _____ *him.*

2. How would you define the word *compassion*?

3. Find a story in the Gospel of John where Jesus showed compassion to someone. _____

   _____

   _____

   _____

   _____

4. Besides widows and orphans, what other groups of people do you feel need compassion? Explain. _____

   _____

   _____

   _____

   _____

   _____

   _____

❄ Hear God's Voice

The Lord is full of compassion and mercy.

—*James 5:11*

❄ Live It Out

This week I will be God's hand of compassion to others by _____

_____

_____

_____

_____

_____

_____

_____

❋ WRITE IT DOWN

Describe a situation where someone showed you compassion when you really needed it. Did it help? Describe how it made you feel about that person. Describe how it made you feel about God. Jot down some ideas about how you can nurture sensitivity and compassion for others in your life.

Week 25
Patience

RACE WITH TIME

It seems like I'm always in a race with time. Do you ever feel like that? Time is such a fickle master, isn't it? I mean, it's never satisfied. When I was a little girl, I wanted to wear makeup before I was old enough. I wanted to drive before I was old enough. I wanted to grow up before it was time. When we become adults, the race with time continues. We want everything faster—quicker microwaves, faster fast food, and shorter shortcuts. Hurry, hurry, hurry! What's the urgency? What's the hurry? Why are we so impatient?

Being the human speed dynamo that I am, I often become impatient with God. I want Him to walk at my pace. I want Him to do things according to my busy schedule. I want Him to answer all my prayers, my way, and on my time. I've even been so impatient at times that I've tried to answer my own prayers. Guess what happens every time I do that!

When we keep our eyes on Jesus, staying in step with Him, we stay steady on our course. Our restless feet can't get us into trouble. Then we can fully enjoy all His blessings. Ask God to give you patience to wait for His perfect timing.

Get into the Word

1. Read Hebrews 6:12 and fill in the blanks: _____ *those who through _____ and _____ inherit what has been promised.*

2. If God is all-powerful, why can't He give us what we need right away? Why do we need patience? _____

   _____

   _____

   _____

3. What do you think faith has to do with patience? _____

   _____

   _____

   _____

4. What do you think the verse above means when it refers to "what has been promised"? _____

   _____

   _____

   _____

   _____

❄ HEAR GOD'S VOICE

Learn to be patient, so that you will please God and be given what he has promised.

—*Hebrews 10:36 CEV*

❄ LIVE IT OUT

This week I will practice the power of patience by _____

_____

_____

_____

_____

_____

_____

_____

✿ WRITE IT DOWN

Describe a situation in your life when you had to wait patiently for something you really wanted. What emotions did you experience while you were waiting? How do you think waiting patiently for *God's* promises will feel the same? How do you think it will feel different?

_____

_____

_____

_____

_____

_____

_____

_____

_____

_____

_____

_____

Week 26
Sex

❧ LOOKING FOR LOVE

Satan has a tricky way of turning down our "sin-sensitivity" level. You know what I mean. The first time you step over a line, you feel that twinge of guilt in your stomach, telling you that what you're doing isn't right. But the next time you do it, you're not quite so sensitive to the conviction. It gets easier to ignore, and pretty soon you don't feel it at all.

The Bible says that sexual sin is different from any other kind of sin: "Run away from sexual sin! No other sin so clearly affects the body as this one does. For sexual immorality is a sin against your own body" (1 Corinthians 6:18 NLT). It's different because when we share that kind of intimacy with another person, we become "one" with that person; but God wants us to be one spirit with *Him* (see 1 Corinthians 6:16–17).

Make sure you are looking for love in the right place. I encourage you to think about what is most important to you. Talk to God about it. Ask Him to help you make Him first in your life. It's a daily effort of seeking Him. The good news is that He is always pursuing you—and He will never stop.

❋ GET INTO THE WORD

1. Read 1 Corinthians 6:19–20 and fill in the blanks: *Do you not know that your _____ is a _____ of the Holy Spirit, who is in you, whom you have received from God? You are not your _____; you were bought at a _____. Therefore _____ God with your _____.*

2. What do you think the verse above means when it says your body is a "temple of the Holy Spirit"? _____

   _____

   _____

   _____

3. What do you think it means to sin against your own body? _____

   _____

   _____

   _____

4. How will closeness with God help you to avoid sexual sin? _____

   _____

   _____

   _____

   _____

✿ HEAR GOD'S VOICE

Guard the treasure you were given!
Guard it with your life.

—*1 Timothy 6:20* MSG

✿ LIVE IT OUT

This week I will make a positive effort to avoid sexual sin by _____

_____

_____

_____

_____

_____

_____

_____

❀ WRITE IT DOWN

Describe how it makes you feel to know that your body is a temple. Does it make you feel beautiful? Holy? Describe some guidelines you feel are realistic that can help you honor your body in the way God asks.

Week 27
God's Presence

✿ No Words

Just the other day I was driving down I-65, feeling overwhelmed by a lot of piddly decisions I needed to make. All these thoughts were flooding my mind, and I felt extremely alone. Just when I felt my head was about to explode, something incredible happened. I felt an overpowering sense of God's presence. I was intensely aware that "faith, hope, and love is more than enough when times get tough." I was completely filled with an unexpected, wonderful peace.

I didn't ask for it—I didn't have the presence of mind to ask for it—but suddenly, the peace that passes understanding surrounded me. I could feel it in every fiber of my being. I was not alone. God was right there with me in my car. My sovereign God knew the exact moment I needed His hand to gently stroke my head and fill my heart with peace.

When I finally acknowledged His almighty presence, I could find no words to express my gratitude to Him. My nose started to sting, and tears poured from my eyes. The God of everything went out of His way to allow me to experience His presence. He'll do the same for you.

🌸 GET INTO THE WORD

1. Read Psalm 16:11 and fill in the blanks: *You have made known to me the path of _____; you will fill me with _____ in your _____, with eternal _____ at your right hand.*

2. If God is always with us, why don't we always feel His presence?

   _____

   _____

   _____

   _____

   _____

3. If Jesus is seated at the right hand of God the Father, who is it that brings us the presence of God?_____

   _____

   _____

   _____

   _____

   _____

   _____

   _____

❋ HEAR GOD'S VOICE

Blessed are those who have learned to acclaim you,
who walk in the light of your presence, O LORD.
They rejoice in your name all day long.

—*Psalm 89:15–16*

❋ LIVE IT OUT

This week I will demonstrate that I desire to be in God's presence by

_____

_____

_____

_____

_____

_____

_____

_____

❀ WRITE IT DOWN

Describe in detail how you think it must feel to be in God's presence.
Can you recall a time when you felt the presence of God with you?
Explain.

_____

_____

_____

_____

_____

_____

_____

_____

_____

_____

_____

_____

_____

_____

Unity

❋ OUR TESTIMONY OF LOVE

Jesus prays a beautiful prayer in John 17. It is partly a prayer about friendship. He begins by praying for His dear friends, His disciples. He asks God to keep them safe, to prepare their way, and to give them power in His name. Then He turns His attention toward future believers— that's us. Stop for just a minute to think about the significance of this prayer. Two thousand years ago, Jesus prayed for you and me. That's incredible! And do you know what He prayed *for*? He prayed that we would be *one*.

If you knew that you had only a few days left on this earth, how would it affect the way you relate to other people? Would you choose your words more carefully?

Think of a fellow believer you have a hard time loving. Now think of what Jesus intends your unity with him or her to accomplish. When we look at it that way, it becomes evident that it's much more important to glorify God than to win an argument. If we can value our unity above our selfish desires, those around us will see the testimony of our love and come to understand how much God loves them.

1 Read Colossians 3:12–14 and fill in the blanks: *As God's
_____ people, holy and dearly loved, clothe yourselves with
compassion, kindness, humility, gentleness and _____. Bear
with each other and _____ whatever grievances you may have
against one another. Forgive as the Lord forgave you. And over all
these _____ put on love, which _____ them all together
in perfect _____.*

2. Why would it be God's desire for us to get along with one another?

_____

_____

_____

_____

_____

3. List the good qualities in the verse above that lead to unity.

_____

_____

_____

_____

❋ Hear God's Voice

How good and pleasant it is
when God's people live together in peace!
—*Psalm 133:1 NIrV*

❋ Live It Out

This week I will take a step toward being in unity with someone I have
clashed with in the past by _____

_____

_____

_____

_____

_____

✳ WRITE IT DOWN

Describe what you think would happen if all Christians were in unity with one another. How do you think our homes would be changed? Our churches? Our world? Do you have any ideas that would encourage unity among the Christians you know?

_____

_____

_____

_____

_____

_____

_____

_____

_____

_____

_____

Prayer

ACTS

When I talk about prayer, I'm talking about more than the prayers you pray with other people listening in. It is also more than asking God for things—even when we're asking for other people. Prayer is about getting to know God.

Let me share with you the first formula I learned when I was growing up, based on the word ACTS.

- *A* is for *adoration*, which is praising God and telling Him how truly awesome He is and how much you love Him.
- *C* is for *confession*. When you confess your sins to God, be as specific as you possibly can. You'll be more aware of your weakness and better able to ask for God's help. And make sure that you not only confess but also repent of, or turn away from, your sin.
- *T* is for *thanksgiving*. Thank the Lord for all the many blessings that He gives you daily. Again, be specific, because not only does it bless God's heart, it opens your eyes to how great He is.
- *S* is for *supplication*. Supplication is humbly asking God to help you with your personal needs and the needs of others.

❁ Get into the Word

1. Read Philippians 4:6–7 and fill in the blanks: *Do not be _____ about anything, but in everything, by prayer and _____, with _____, present your requests to God. And the _____ of God, which _____ all understanding, will guard your hearts and your _____ in Christ Jesus.*

2. What are the four ACTS of prayer? Which form of prayer do you use most? _____
   _____
   _____

3. How does asking God for the things you need create peace in your heart?_____
   _____
   _____
   _____

4. The verse above says that prayer will bring peace, and peace will guard your heart. What does it guard against? _____
   _____
   _____
   _____

❋ HEAR GOD'S VOICE

When you call on me, when you come and pray to me, I'll listen. When you come looking for me, you'll find me.

—Jeremiah 29:12–13 MSG

❋ LIVE IT OUT

This week I will encourage prayer in my own life and the lives of my friends by asking several of my friends to pray with me about _____

_____

_____

_____

_____

_____

_____

❀ WRITE IT DOWN

How do you feel about talking to God in prayer? What emotions do you feel when you pray? Describe a time when you prayed about something and it was answered in a dramatic way. How did that increase your faith in God?

_____

_____

_____

_____

_____

_____

_____

_____

_____

_____

_____

Week 30
Obedience

🌼 His Way

The Bible makes it clear that obedience isn't an option. Ephesians 6:1 says, "Children, obey your parents in the Lord, for this is right." It doesn't say, "Children, obey your parents when it's easy," or, "Children, obey your parents if you agree with them." It pretty much just says, "Obey."

This may seem so cut-and-dried—unreasonable, almost—but we need to understand that God didn't give us these commands to make our teenage years miserable. He is interested in protecting us just as much or more than our parents are. We are His *children*, and He loves us as only a perfect Father can. So even when it's really hard and we don't understand, we have to trust God and obey Him. And even when we don't agree, if we love Him, we will keep His commandments.

Life is not about getting our way. It's about pleasing God and doing things His way. So . . . in the situations that seem like a huge deal and in the little everyday things of life, our parents deserve our obedience. For you as a young woman trying to follow Christ, honoring and obeying your mom and dad are some of the most important things you can do to show your love for Him.

1. Read Titus 3:1 and fill in the blanks: *Remind the people to be _____ to rulers and _____, to be _____, to be ready to do whatever is _____.*

2. Why do you think it is sometimes difficult to be obedient? _____

   _____

   _____

   _____

3. Would God ever ask us to do something that is obviously wrong—lie, cheat, or steal, for example? How do you know?_____

   _____

   _____

   _____

   _____

4. What tools has God given you to help you become obedient? Read 2 Timothy 3 and Philippians 4. _____

   _____

   _____

   _____

   _____

🌸 HEAR GOD'S VOICE

Although [Jesus] was [God's] son, he learned obedience from what he suffered and, once made perfect, he became the source of eternal salvation for all who obey him.

—Hebrews 5:8–9

🌸 LIVE IT OUT

This week I will demonstrate a willingness to be obedient in an area of my life where I have previously not been willing by _____

_____

_____

_____

_____

_____

_____

❉ Write It Down

Describe a specific situation where someone asked you to do something, and you were obedient. Describe another situation when you weren't obedient. How do you feel about those situations now? Would you choose differently now? Explain why you think God is so concerned about your obeying even in the little details of life.

Life

❀ STORMS OF LIFE

Do you remember when Peter saw Jesus walking on the stormy waters to His disciples' boat? Peter asked to walk on the water to meet Him, and Jesus said, "Come." As long as Peter kept his eyes focused on Jesus, he stayed on top of the water. But when he took his eyes off Jesus and began to look at the wind and the waves, he began to sink. Jesus reached out His hand, caught him, and brought him to safety.

Aren't we a lot like Peter? One minute we believe God is with us and that we can do all things. The next minute we take our eyes off Him, focus on the waves around us—and we begin to doubt that the God of the universe can handle our problems.

As you struggle through the waves of life, remember to keep your eyes focused on Jesus. When the roar of the waves in your ears threatens to drown out the sound of His voice, listen all the harder, and you will hear Him say, "You can do it! I'm right here!" And then when you reach the other side of the stormy waters, He'll pull you into His arms and tell you how much He loves you and how proud of you He is.

🌸 GET INTO THE WORD

1. Read Psalm 91:14–15 (NIrv) and fill in the blanks: *The Lord says, "I will save the one who _____ me. I will keep him safe, because he trusts in me. He will _____ out to me, and I will answer him. I will be with him in times of _____. I will _____ him and _____ him."*

2. Who causes the storms in our lives? God? Satan? The behavior of others? Our own foolishness? Explain your answer. _____

   _____

   _____

   _____

   _____

   _____

3. What does the verse above instruct us to do when we find ourselves in a stormy circumstance? _____

   _____

   _____

   _____

   _____

   _____

HEAR GOD'S VOICE

[Jesus said]: "In this world you will have trouble. But take heart! I have overcome the world."

—*John 16:33*

LIVE IT OUT

This week I will demonstrate my willingness to trust God in a particularly stormy circumstance in my life by _____

_____

_____

_____

_____

_____

_____

❈ WRITE IT DOWN

Describe the stormy circumstance you or a friend might be experiencing right now. What do you think God is trying to say through the thunder of the waves? What makes this a good opportunity to demonstrate your faith and trust in God's love and faithfulness?

_____

_____

_____

_____

_____

_____

_____

_____

_____

_____

_____

Truth

🌸 Jesus Is

We have a special friend who I'll call Mary. She is one of the sweetest, coolest, most complimentary people you could ever meet. We met her a long time ago when she did our hair and makeup for a photo shoot. Mary has a psychic whom she relies on for the big decisions in her life. It's really been hard for me to know what to say to Mary when her psychic comes up in conversation.

Looking to psychics or black magic or even horoscopes to find guidance for life is a slap in the face of God. He is our Father. Why would we turn to anyone else?

The reason I love the song "Jesus Is" so much is that it is pure Scripture—no fancy words or metaphors, just the basics. God's truth is simple. We just have to open our mouths and say the words: Jesus is "the way, the truth, and the life." Like the song says, the noise in this world is so loud that we've got to be a still, small voice speaking the truth boldly and in love. Until we spread the Word, lost people will continue to seek answers from empty sources. We know the truth; let's tell the world in a gentle voice that Jesus is.

❋ GET INTO THE WORD

1. Read 1 Timothy 2:3–5 (NCV) and fill in the blanks: *God our Savior . . . wants _____ people to be _____ and he wants everyone to know the _____. There is only one _____ and there is only one _____ that people can reach _____. That way is through Jesus Christ, who is also a _____.*

2. Why is it so important to stand up for the truth about Jesus Christ being the only way to fellowship with God the Father? _____

    _____

    _____

    _____

3. Name two important ways you can know that Jesus is the truth.

    _____

    _____

    _____

    _____

    _____

    _____

    _____

✿ HEAR GOD'S VOICE

Jesus answered, "I am the way and the truth and the life."

—*John 14:6*

✿ LIVE IT OUT

This week I will tell someone the reasons why I know that there is only one God, and Jesus is the only way we can meet Him and have fellowship with Him. _____

_____

_____

_____

_____

_____

❋ WRITE IT DOWN

Imagine that you are standing on a hillside, and many people of different races and cultures are listening to you. How would you convince them that Jesus is the only way for them to know their heavenly Father? How would you feel if they left unconvinced? Describe how you would feel if they received your words as truth.

Marriage

❋ Worth the Wait

Are you imagining what your future husband will be like? You will have to wait to find out—some longer than others. But I promise you it will be worth the wait. I'll never forget hearing Heather talk about her spiritual struggles before she met Brian. She was going through a difficult time of questioning. The three of us were happily married, and she didn't even have a prospect.

One day, on her knees, crying out to the Lord, she finally came to the realization that God wanted some special time with just her. She made the choice to focus on and nurture her relationship with Him. And of course, not too long after that, Brian came into the picture.

I'm often amazed at how God works. Look back to Adam and Eve. "For Adam no suitable helper was found." But God had a plan all along. God put Adam into a deep sleep and gave him the perfect mate. I am just as guilty as you may be of trying to make things happen instead of trusting the Lord and waiting on Him. It's not always easy to wait—I know Heather would testify to that. But she would also testify that God was right in the end.

✤ GET INTO THE WORD

1. Read 1 Corinthians 7:32 (MSG) and fill in the blanks: *When you're _____, you're free to concentrate on simply _____ the _____. . . . All I want is for you to be able to develop a way of _____ in which you can spend plenty of time together with the Master without a lot of _____.*

2. What advantages do you see in being married over being single?

    _____

    _____

    _____

    _____

    _____

3. What advantages do you see in allowing God to choose your husband for you? _____

    _____

    _____

    _____

    _____

    _____

    _____

✿ HEAR GOD'S VOICE

If we hope for what we don't already have, we wait for it patiently.

—*Romans 8:24*

✿ LIVE IT OUT

This week I will go out with my friends and have fun, consciously thinking of the guys I meet simply as friends rather than potential husbands. Instead, I will take a step toward trusting God to provide a husband for me by

_____

_____

_____

_____

_____

_____

✾ Write It Down

Describe the man you would like to marry. What characteristics are most important to you? What characteristics are you developing that would make you a good wife? Tell God how you will feel if it is His plan for you to remain unmarried.

God's Mercy

❋ It's a Mystery

We always set up a booth for Mercy Ministries at our concerts and say something from the stage about the help they give to hurting girls. As we did final preparations for a concert in North Carolina, we realized we had left all the brochures behind. We considered doing nothing, but decided to have Denise share what Mercy Ministries is all about.

What we didn't know was that there was a young girl in the audience who desperately needed to hear about God's mercy and needed to hear it quickly. Just that day, she had found out she was pregnant. Unmarried and a teenager, she surely felt her situation was insurmountable.

As Denise shared about Mercy Ministries that night, the Holy Spirit did a work in that young girl's life. After the concert, she came through the autograph line and inconspicuously asked for Mercy's Special Help Line (1-800-922-9131).

It's a mystery to me how God guides our hearts to make decisions that allow His love to shine through. But I saw the divine providence of God at work that night. And you can believe it is at work in and through your life too.

GET INTO THE WORD

1. Read Hebrews 4:15–16 and fill in the blanks: *We do not have a high _____ who is unable to sympathize with our _____, but we have one who has been tempted in every way, just as we are—yet without _____. Let us then approach the throne of grace with _____, so that we may receive _____ and find grace to help us in our time of _____.*

2. How does it help to know that Jesus understands our temptations and our failings? _____

   _____

   _____

3. How can prayer make us more sensitive to the needs of others? ___

   _____

   _____

   _____

4. How does God guide us to demonstrate His mercy to others? ___

   _____

   _____

   _____

   _____

🌸 HEAR GOD'S VOICE

You are the ones chosen by God . . . to be a holy people, God's instruments to do his work and speak out for him, to tell others of the night-and-day difference he made for you—from nothing to something, from rejected to accepted.

—*1 Peter 2:10 MSG*

🌸 LIVE IT OUT

This week I will reach out to someone who is in need of God's mercy by

_____

_____

_____

_____

_____

_____

_____

❋ WRITE IT DOWN

Describe a situation when you needed God's mercy and He provided it for you. How did it make you feel to know that God cared for you? Describe a situation where a friend needed God's mercy. Did you respond? How? What was the end result?

Victory

✳ WE WIN!

Have you ever watched a rerun of a ball game when you already knew the outcome, and you knew your team won? The others watching the game, who don't know the outcome, are going completely bonkers! They're screaming and yelling and getting all worked up. You, on the other hand, are calm and collected. Your team might fall apart and have a bad quarter, but you know that eventually, things are going to turn around. You may get a little nervous watching the bad parts, but you are calmed by the expectant hope and knowledge that your team is going to win.

The same principle applies to the Christian walk. We know how the game turns out. The message of the Bible is that we win! Everything around you may be falling apart. You may lose your cool and get angry with a friend or family member. You may get so depressed. But, my friend, what happened at the cross declares victory to all believers. Satan, the prince of this world, is powerless in the light of God's love.

❋ GET INTO THE WORD

1. Read Proverbs 2:7–8 and fill in the blanks: *[The LORD] holds
   _____ in store for the _____, he is a shield to those whose
   walk is _____, for he guards the course of the _____ and
   _____ the way of his faithful ones.*

2. How did Jesus defeat Satan? _____
   _____
   _____
   _____

3. Does God see us as blameless in our Christian walk because we
   always do what's right, or because Jesus always did what was right?
   Explain your answer. _____
   _____
   _____
   _____

4. What does the verse above tell us about God's commitment to us?
   _____
   _____
   _____
   _____

🌸 HEAR GOD'S VOICE

Since future victory is sure, be strong and steady, always abounding in the Lord's work.

—*1 Corinthians 15:58 TLB*

🌸 LIVE IT OUT

This week I will demonstrate the victory I have in Jesus by asking for and receiving His forgiveness when I mess up. And I will remind Satan that he is defeated and no longer has any power over me.

_____

_____

_____

_____

_____

Describe a situation where you avoided sin by trusting in the Lord and demonstrated your victory over our enemy—Satan. How did you feel when you were going through it? How did you feel afterward? How can knowing that Satan has been defeated help you in future situations?

Week 36
God's Promises

❋ TOGETHER FOR GOOD

God works all things together for good. Even though God cares very much for us, bad things still happen. I don't know all the answers to why God allows our parents to divorce, our dads to walk out, abuse to take place, or innocent children to suffer for things that are totally out of their control. I do know Satan has *some* power in this world, and I know that all the evil in this world originates with him.

But God has *ultimate* power. Though Satan brings pain and suffering into the world, the Bible promises that God will ultimately bring good from the pain we face in life.

There will be times in your life when you experience pain you never thought possible. There will be times when bad things will happen to you. At those times, you must reach out and claim God's promises. You must believe that He is weaving all the circumstances of your life into a gorgeous tapestry. On the backside, you can see mistakes and backstitches and ugly knots, but on the front, you see a beautiful arrangement of color and design.

❋ GET INTO THE WORD

1. Read Romans 8:28 (NLT) and fill in the blanks: *We _____ that God causes _____ to work together for the _____ of those who love God and are called according to his _____ for them.*

2. What does God promise to do with the pain we suffer in our lives?

   _____

   _____

   _____

3. Name three godly character traits you believe can be developed when we are suffering. Explain your answer. _____

   _____

   _____

   _____

4. God's promises are good how much of the time? How can we be sure? _____

   _____

   _____

   _____

✽ HEAR GOD'S VOICE

*Our light and momentary troubles are achieving for us
an eternal glory that far outweighs them all.*

—*2 Corinthians 4:17*

✽ LIVE IT OUT

This week I will bring the pain that is dogging my life and give it to the
Lord. I will then demonstrate my trust in His promises by _____

_____

_____

_____

_____

_____

_____

❋ WRITE IT DOWN

Describe a situation in your life when God has kept a promise to you in an obvious way. Do you believe He still keeps His promises? Why or why not? Do you believe He can bring something good from the pain you are feeling right now? Tell Him why.

_____

_____

_____

_____

_____

_____

_____

_____

_____

_____

_____

Week 37

Dating

To Date or Not to Date

High school can be such a fun part of life, so why does dating have to complicate everything so much? It goes back to the issue of what we are searching for and who we find our security in. The problem is that being intimate (kissing, hugging, holding hands, and a lot more) has become so common with young people that it seems odd when that's not part of a relationship. Is there something wrong with just being great friends? Can't you still go out to movies, football games, and concerts? We often think we have to do more.

I realized that what really matters is not whether I date or not—what really matters is, *Am I listening to God? Am I glorifying Him in my relationships?* This means it's not even about guys, it's more about how we love and respect others—all others.

As I think back over the guys I dated, I realize that that question didn't even enter my mind. I never asked, "Lord, how can a relationship with this guy draw me closer to You, and how can I show him how great You are?" If we would put on the mind of Christ in any relationship, imagine how much more we would care for others.

GET INTO THE WORD

1. Read Romans 6:13 and fill in the blanks: *Do not offer the parts of your _____ to sin, as instruments of _____, but rather offer _____ to God, as those who have been _____ from death to life; and offer the parts of your body to him as instruments of _____.*

2. Why do you think God is concerned about who we date, even if we aren't planning to marry that person? Explain your answer.____

   _____

   _____

   _____

3. Why is it more important to respect the guys we date than to simply be attracted by their good looks and personality? _____

   _____

   _____

   _____

4. What are your guidelines for dating? _____

   _____

   _____

   _____

�֍ HEAR GOD'S VOICE

Whatever you do, do it all for the glory of God.
—*1 Corinthians 10:31 NLT*

✷ LIVE IT OUT

This week I will get together with my friends and suggest that we work together to develop godly guidelines for dating.

_____

_____

_____

_____

_____

_____

_____

❋ WRITE IT DOWN

Describe your idea of a perfect date. Would you be comfortable knowing that Jesus was on your date with you? Why or why not? Does this concept change your idea of a perfect date? In what ways?

_____

_____

_____

_____

_____

_____

_____

_____

_____

_____

_____

_____

_____

Bible Reading

❋ TELL ME HOW

You probably know you should be reading the Bible every day—but I'd like to do more than tell you what you should do. Here are some practical ideas to help you get started:

- **Daily devotional books** have a scripture reading every day and then a devotional thought based on the passage.

- **The book of Proverbs** contains 31 chapters—one for each day of the month. When you get to the end, you can just start over.

- **The book of Psalms** has 150 chapters. You can read a psalm a day for five months without repeating.

- **The whole Bible** might sound daunting, but I challenge you to set the goal of reading the Bible all the way through. It takes a while, and there are some difficult passages, but it is altogether a wonderful experience. Try an easy-to-read version like the New Living Translation.

You'll find that the more you read the Bible on a daily basis, the more you will work out your own system of doing it. What is important is that you do it consistently.

1. Read James 1:25 and fill in the blanks: *The man who looks _____ _____ into the perfect law that gives _____, and continues to do this, not _____ what he has heard, but _____ it—he will be _____ in what he does.*

2. Why is it important to read the Bible daily?_____
   _____
   _____
   _____
   _____

3. What is the advantage of reading from different parts of the Bible rather than passages that are familiar to us? _____
   _____
   _____
   _____
   _____
   _____
   _____

❋ HEAR GOD'S VOICE

I will study your teachings
and follow your footsteps.
I will take pleasure in your laws
and remember your words.

—*Psalm 119:15–16* CEV

❋ LIVE IT OUT

This week I will ask an adult close to me to be my Bible-reading monitor, someone who will check on me regularly to ensure that I'm reading consistently, someone who will challenge me to set and keep reading goals.

_____

_____

_____

_____

_____

❋ WRITE IT DOWN

Describe how you feel about the reading ideas on page 152. Which one sounds the most interesting to you? Why? Which one will be the greatest challenge? Why?

_____

_____

_____

_____

_____

_____

_____

_____

_____

_____

_____

_____

self-image

❀ GET INTO SHAPE

God has created each of us with our own unique set of gifts and abilities, our own personalities, and our own special looks. The trouble is that many girls aren't satisfied with the shape God has given them. Surprisingly, even the most beautiful models say they would like to change something about themselves. How do you feel about the way God shaped you?

Before you answer, think about this. God has shaped you in a unique way to serve Him. He has special things in mind for you. In the book of Isaiah, God says, "The people I formed for myself that they may proclaim my praise" (43:21). It's pretty hard to broadcast God's praises when you aren't happy with the way He created you. But you can become happy when you understand the beauty of your own unique shape. In Rick Warren's book *The Purpose Driven Life*, he makes the word *shape* into an acronym.

Spiritual gifts • **H**eart • **A**bilities • **P**ersonality • **E**xperience

You have been given each of the features above—hand-selected by God just for you—to be used for Him.

❀ GET INTO THE WORD

1. Read Psalm 139:13–14 and fill in the blanks: *You _____ my inmost being; you knit me together in my mother's _____. I _____ you because I am fearfully and _____ made; your works are _____, I know that full well.*

2. Name the five elements of SHAPE. _____
    _____
    _____
    _____

3. Are there any that you have not thought about until now? Which ones? Which are your strengths? _____
    _____
    _____
    _____

4. How do these elements make you different from anyone else in the universe, completely unique? _____
    _____
    _____
    _____
    _____

Your hands shaped me and made me.

—*Job 10:8*

❋ LIVE IT OUT

This week I will identify at least five characteristics that make me a good person and a good friend. I will write them down and hang them in a place in my room where I will see them every day. As I identify others, I will add them to the list. _____

_____

_____

_____

_____

_____

❋ WRITE IT DOWN

Describe your two best friends in terms of their SHAPE. How does this process cause you to love, respect, and appreciate them more? Be specific.

_____

_____

_____

_____

_____

_____

_____

_____

_____

_____

_____

_____

_____

_____

_____

God's Peace

❀ LIFE IS SHORT

When we first came together as Point of Grace, fresh out of college, we didn't feel we had much to share. We were young and inexperienced, and we hadn't encountered much of life. But one thing we had experienced was the love of God. And with each passing year, we come to know His love even more.

I've found that God often shows His love for us through the peace He gives us. I don't know about you, but I'm a very worried and stressed-out person most of the time. Often, when I'm driving in my car or alone with my thoughts, my mind begins to fill with all sorts of concerns. One worry leads to another, and in five minutes my peace with myself and with God is completely gone.

I've been challenging myself lately to remember that life is short, that none of the things I'm worrying about really have any eternal consequence, and that God loves me. When I think on these things, almost always, He calms my mind and brings me peace. I see that He cares for my smallest concerns, my irrational worried thoughts, and replaces them with comfort, love, and peace.

✿ GET INTO THE WORD

1. Read Isaiah 32:17–18 and fill in the blanks: *The fruit of righteousness will be _____; the effect of righteousness will be _____ and confidence forever. My people will live in _____ dwelling places, in secure homes, in _____ places of rest.*

2. What does a lack of peace in our lives say about our trust in God?

   _____

   _____

   _____

3. What are your three greatest worries? _____

   _____

   _____

   _____

4. Will any of these still be a problem in one year, two years, five years? _____

   _____

   _____

   _____

   _____

🌸 Hear God's Voice

You, Lord, give true peace. You give peace to those who depend on you. You give peace to those who trust you.

—*Isaiah 26:3 NCV*

🌸 Live It Out

This week I will allow God's love to help me release my worries and fears and receive His peace by _____

_____

_____

_____

_____

_____

_____

WRITE IT DOWN

Describe what it means to you to know that God is bigger than any anxiety or worry you might have. Describe how you see God resolving your three greatest worries. What should your role be in exchanging your anxiety for God's peace?

_____

_____

_____

_____

_____

_____

_____

_____

_____

_____

_____

_____

Week 41
Talents and Gifts

❋ GIFTS OF GRACE

According to Rick Warren, spiritual gifts are special gifts given only to Christians and given for the express purpose of serving God. Here's how the apostle Paul explains it in Ephesians: "Christ gave each one of us the special gift of grace, showing how generous he is. And Christ gave gifts to people—he made some to be apostles, some to be prophets, some to go and tell the Good News, and some to have the work of caring for and teaching God's people. Christ gave those gifts to prepare God's holy people for the work of serving, to make the body of Christ stronger" (4:7, 11–12 NCV).

God has given you spiritual gifts too. You may have the gift of making people feel comfortable or the ability to see into people's hearts and sympathize with their hurts. Your gift might be encouragement or generosity or sharing your faith. Maybe you have the gift of leadership. Whatever gift God has given you, He intends that you use it for Him. Sometimes it takes us a while to figure out what our spiritual gifts are—and that's okay. Ask God to show you where you fit in. You'll figure it out with a little time, prayer, and patience.

❀ GET INTO THE WORD

1. Read 1 Peter 4:10–11 and fill in the blanks: *Each one should use whatever _____ he has received to serve others, faithfully administering God's _____ in its various forms. If anyone speaks, he should do it as one _____ the very words of God. If anyone serves, he should do it with the _____ God provides, so that in all things _____ may be praised through Jesus Christ.*

2. What is the primary reason God has given us spiritual gifts? Explain. _____

   _____

   _____

   _____

3. Can you identify any spiritual gifts in your life? What are they?

   _____

   _____

   _____

   _____

   _____

   _____

✿ Hear God's Voice

You each have your own gift from God. One has this gift. Another has that.

—*1 Corinthians 7:7 NIrV*

✿ Live It Out

This week I will identify at least one spiritual gift that operates in my life, and I will use it by _____

_____

_____

_____

_____

_____

_____

_____

🌼 WRITE IT DOWN

Describe the spiritual gifts you see in your closest friends. How do they glorify God and serve all of God's people? What are some ways you can encourage your friends to use their spiritual gifts? How can they encourage you to use yours?

_____

_____

_____

_____

_____

_____

_____

_____

_____

_____

_____

Week 42
God's Grace

❀ SAVING GRACE

We are quick to judge people who look different, smell different, act different, or come from a different background. When God places a person in your life who is difficult to love, try to remember that you don't know where he or she has come from or what difficulties brought that person to the current situation.

God reminds us of the value of reaching out to those whom society shuns—pregnant teenagers, kids on drugs, teens living on the streets. As you share God's grace through a life lived in love, you become His hands, His feet, His voice—to people desperately in need of love.

It's all about getting your hands dirty helping the hurting, so they can see that Christ has saving grace and love for them. They'll never believe us if we don't reach out and love them exactly as they are.

Just the other day, I heard a preacher say, "When it's all said and done, there are only two kinds of people in the world—saved and unsaved." It's my hope that we can live love in a way that demonstrates God's saving grace to lost and hurting souls.

🌼 GET INTO THE WORD

1. Read Titus 3:5–7 and fill in the blanks. *[God, our Savior]*
   _____ *us, not because of righteous things we had done, but*
   because of his _____. He saved us through the washing of
   rebirth and _____ by the Holy Spirit, whom he poured out
   on us generously through Jesus Christ our _____, so that,
   having been justified by his grace, we might become _____
   having the hope of eternal life.

2. After reading the above verse, what do you think the word *grace*
   means? _____

   _____

   _____

3. Why do we need God's grace in our lives? _____

   _____

   _____

4. According to the last part of the verse above, what does God's
   grace provide for us? _____

   _____

   _____

🌸 HEAR GOD'S VOICE

God is so rich in mercy, and he loved us so much, that even though we were dead because of our sins, he gave us life when he raised Christ from the dead. (It is only by God's grace that you have been saved!)

—*Ephesians 2:4–5 NLT*

🌸 LIVE IT OUT

This week I will thank God for His grace in my life and demonstrate God's grace to someone else by _____

_____

_____

_____

_____

_____

_____

❋ WRITE IT DOWN

Grace has been defined as: **G**od's **R**ighteousness **A**t **C**hrist's **E**xpense. What do you think this means in regard to your Christian walk? Describe a situation when you know His grace was poured out on you. Write a little prayer thanking Him for His grace.

Suffering

🌸 WHYS

I don't know all the answers to why we have to suffer in this life, but I do know that if it never rained, we wouldn't know how to appreciate the beautiful sunshine. If we never experienced pain, we wouldn't know the joy of relief. Though we can't answer all the *whys*, we can know that His grace in our lives will make everything right.

No matter how dreary things may look, our God will work everything together for good. Even if in this life we don't see the physical victory, we remain confident that better days are ahead, for our hope is based not on what we can see but on the unseen.

Hold steady while you wait for better days—they will come! Keep your spiritual eyes focused on the *unseen* hope, and don't get depressed by looking at the *seen* despair. Ask God to forgive you when you doubt His love, His desire, and His ability to bring you through. Praise Him for His promise to give you better days. Remember the words of this old song: "My hope is built on nothing less than Jesus' blood and righteousness."

❧ GET INTO THE WORD

1. Read James 1:12 and fill in the blanks: _____ *is the man who*
    _____ *under trial, because when he has stood the test, he will*
    _____ *the crown of _____ that God has _____ to*
    those who love him.

2. Why do you think there is suffering in the world? _____
    _____
    _____
    _____

3. Do you think it is possible for us to grow spiritually from
    suffering? How? _____
    _____
    _____
    _____

4. What is God's commitment to us when we are suffering?_____
    _____
    _____
    _____
    _____
    _____

🌸 HEAR GOD'S VOICE

What we are suffering now is nothing compared with the glory that will be shown in us.

—Romans 8:18

🌸 LIVE IT OUT

This week I will quietly encourage someone I know who is in pain by

_____

_____

_____

_____

_____

_____

_____

❋ WRITE IT DOWN

Describe a time when you were really hurting and God sent someone to encourage and comfort you. Write a prayer to God thanking Him for His love and grace. Think about what other people in your life are going through right now. Write a prayer asking God to use you to bring encouragement to their lives.

Week 44
Quiet Time

🌼 TIME WITH GOD

When I was a young teenager, someone challenged me to begin having a personal devotional or quiet time with God every day. During the first few weeks, it was really hard to make the time. But I was determined, and so every day I would read the Bible, pray, and write in my journal. Before I knew it, my time with God was a regular part of my day. Now in my adult life, I see my time with God as a *necessity*. Only by spending time with Him am I able to respond to things in a godly way. Regular time with God is the most enriching and rewarding experience in my life.

I would like to extend the same challenge to you. If you accept this challenge and regularly make time for God in your life, you will be blessed beyond your dreams. And once you make time with Him a habit, you'll find that if you neglect your quiet time, you will miss Him immensely. God is the life-giver and the One who nurtures your soul and lavishes His amazing love on you each day. Going about your day without making Him part of it is saying to Him that you don't need Him.

❋ GET INTO THE WORD

1. Read Psalm 119:58–59 and fill in the blanks: *I have* _____ *your face with all my* _____*; be gracious to me according to your* _____*. I have considered my ways and have turned my* _____ *to your* _____*.*

2. Why is quiet time alone with the Lord so important? _____

   _____

   _____

   _____

   _____

3. Can you name two benefits of spending time alone with the Lord, drawing from the verse above? _____

   _____

   _____

   _____

   _____

   _____

   _____

   _____

❋ HEAR GOD'S VOICE

I'm asking God for one thing, only one thing:
To live with him in his house my whole life long....
That's the only quiet, secure place in a noisy world,
The perfect getaway, from the buzz of traffic.

—*Psalm 27:4* MSG

❋ LIVE IT OUT

This week I will choose a specific time to be alone with God each day, and put it on my schedule with my other appointments.

_____

_____

_____

_____

_____

_____

❋ WRITE IT DOWN

Describe a time when you were alone, and you felt the presence of God very strongly. Did the Lord speak to you? What did He say? How did this divine encounter make you feel? Write a letter just to Him telling Him what it means to you to spend time alone with Him.

_____

_____

_____

_____

_____

_____

_____

_____

_____

_____

_____

Week 45
Guilt

❋ HE UNDERSTANDS

Guilt is one of the worst feelings. I guess that's why Satan likes to use it so much. It begins in a small drawer in a filing cabinet in the back of your mind, and it grows and eats at your soul. You long to be forgiven, but you don't dare tell a soul because you're so filled with shame.

Almost on a daily basis, Point of Grace receives letters in which people share their grief and pain and guilt. Some tell of abortions, others of eating disorders. Some are victims of abuse, drugs, or alcohol. We frequently read things like, "God could never forgive me. I can't tell anyone what I've done. No one would understand." But God *does* forgive, and He *does* understand.

If you feel yourself drowning in guilt, you should know this, my friend. God loves you! Don't be afraid that He will give you a beating. He's not that kind of father. He knows everything about you. He knows your weaknesses and your sin—and He loves you anyway! Go ahead and tell God what you've done and how you feel. He already knows, but He wants you to allow Him to forgive and restore your precious soul.

❀ Get into the Word

1. Read Hebrews 10:22 and fill in the blanks: *Let us draw near to God with a _____ heart in full assurance of _____, having our hearts sprinkled to _____ us from a _____ conscience and having our bodies _____ with pure water.*

2. We feel guilty when we do something wrong. Why do you think that is a good thing? _____

   _____

   _____

   _____

3. What does God want us to do when we feel guilt? _____

   _____

   _____

   _____

4. What does God intend to be the end result of our guilty feelings?

   _____

   _____

   _____

   _____

❋ HEAR GOD'S VOICE

God, create a pure heart in me.
Give me a new spirit that is faithful to you.

—Psalm 51:10 NIrV

❋ LIVE IT OUT

This week I will demonstrate my faith in God by writing out my guilty feelings on a piece of paper. I will go someplace where I am alone with God, ask Him to forgive me for each, and mark through it with a marker. Then I will tear the paper up and throw it away.

_____

_____

_____

_____

_____

❀ WRITE IT DOWN

Describe how it feels to have a guilty conscience. Now describe how it feels to have a conscience washed clean by God. Write a prayer of thanks to God for His love and forgiveness.

_____

_____

_____

_____

_____

_____

_____

_____

_____

_____

_____

Week 46
Divorce

❋ BROKEN PIECES

Your parents' problems are not your fault. It's important that you understand that you have absolutely no control over what happens between your mom and dad. You don't have the power to make them stay married or the power to pull them apart. You only have control over how *you* deal with the broken pieces. We don't get to pick and choose what comes our way, but we do get to choose how we respond.

Maybe your parents are divorced, and you don't have a mom or dad who is there for you. Maybe you've never even known your father or mother. Or maybe your parents are both in your home, but they aren't Christians, and this makes you feel alone.

Whatever your circumstances, God is on your side. With His help, you can turn your circumstances around for good and become more like Jesus in the process. How can living through your parents' divorce make you more like Jesus? I believe that pain can make you stronger in character, more sympathetic to others with similar problems, and more dependent on God, who is the best and most perfect parent we could ever want.

GET INTO THE WORD

1. Read Psalm 34:18 and fill in the blanks: *The LORD is* _____ *to the* _____ *and saves those who are* _____ *in spirit.*

2. What godly character traits do you think could be developed while someone is going through the pain of their parents' divorce? ____

    _____

    _____

    _____

    _____

    _____

3. Do you think divorce was part of God's original plan? Why do you think He allows it? Read Matthew 19. _____

    _____

    _____

    _____

    _____

    _____

    _____

    _____

❀ HEAR GOD'S VOICE

The LORD is good, a strong hold in the day of trouble;
and he knoweth them that trust in him.

—Nahum 1:7 KJV

❀ LIVE IT OUT

This week I will reach out to someone whose parents are divorcing by
sharing some specific word of encouragement that has helped me.

_____

_____

_____

_____

_____

_____

❋ WRITE IT DOWN

Describe how the Lord has comforted you or a close friend while either set of parents went through a divorce. What insights have you gained from the experience?

_____

_____

_____

_____

_____

_____

_____

_____

_____

_____

_____

_____

_____

_____

Week 47
Temptation

THE FIGHT OF YOUR LIFE

Scripture makes this promise: "The temptations that come into your life are no different from what others experience. And God is faithful. He will keep the temptation from becoming so strong that you can't stand up against it. When you are tempted, he will show you a way out so that you will not give in to it" (1 Corinthians 10:13 NLT). What an amazing promise! Whatever temptation you may be experiencing, God has promised a way out. This promise does a couple of things: on the one hand, it gives us tremendous hope; and on the other hand, it takes away our excuses.

If you are struggling to overcome temptation, you may be in the fight of your life. Talk to a trusted adult, a school counselor, a teacher, or another school official. If the first adult you talk to does not get you help, then go to another adult until you find someone who will listen and offer you help. Remember, too, the most significant help you can ever get—whether your secrets are large or small—is found in the blood of Jesus. Only His blood can completely wash away the stains of your hurts, addictions, struggles, and sin.

❉ GET INTO THE WORD

1. Read Ephesians 6:10–12 and fill in the blanks. *Be _____ in the Lord and in his mighty power. Put on the _____ armor of God so that you can take your _____ against the devil's schemes. For our _____ is not against flesh and blood, but against the rulers, against the authorities, against the _____ of this dark world and against the spiritual forces of evil in the heavenly realms.*

2. Why shouldn't you feel guilty about being tempted? _____
   _____
   _____
   _____

3. What does the verse above mean by "armor of God"? Read Ephesians 6:10–18. _____
   _____
   _____
   _____

4. What can you do if you give in to temptation? _____
   _____
   _____
   _____

🌸 Hear God's Voice

Because Jesus himself suffered when he was tempted, he is able to help those who are being tempted.

—Hebrews 2:18

🌸 Live It Out

This week I will ask a friend or loved one to be a kind of sponsor for me, someone I can talk to when I'm feeling tempted. This should be someone strong enough to help me make good choices.

_____

_____

_____

_____

_____

WRITE IT DOWN

Describe a time when you were really tempted to do something you shouldn't, but you resisted. How did you find the strength to overcome? Did you receive help from another person, or did you depend on God alone to help you? Explain. How has that experience helped you with future temptations?

_____

_____

_____

_____

_____

_____

_____

_____

_____

_____

Week 48
Words

🌸 Watch What You Say

One of the guys in our band used to say, "Words that hurt, words that heal," to remind us to watch our mouths whenever the conversation turned gossipy. Our words have mighty power—for good and for bad. And we can't use the excuse that we just "can't help" what we say. For through the power of the Holy Spirit living in us, we really do have the ability to choose how we use our words. As girls striving to become more Christlike, we can actually choose to use our words to help and heal others, instead of to hurt them.

James 1:27 (NLT) says: "If you claim to be religious but don't control your tongue, you are just fooling yourself, and your religion is worthless." These are pretty strong words. James is telling us that even if we are religious in other areas of our lives, if we can't control what we say, our religion is *worthless*. He doesn't say this to discourage us from trying to control our tongues but to remind us that if we can control our tongues, we'll have the discipline to control ourselves in every other way.

GET INTO THE WORD

1. Read Proverbs 12:18, and fill in the blanks. _____ *words pierce like a* _____ *but the tongue of the* _____ *brings* _____.

2. Name three positive things your words can do. _____
   _____
   _____
   _____

3. Who controls the words that come out of your mouth? Explain your answer._____
   _____
   _____
   _____

4. What do you think the writer of the book of James meant when he said, If you don't control your mouth, your religion (your Christianity) is worthless? _____
   _____
   _____
   _____

❋ Hear God's Voice

Be gracious in your speech. The goal is to bring out the best in others in a conversation, not put them down, not cut them out.

—Colossians 4:6 MSG

❋ Live It Out

This week I will take control of my words by _____

_____

_____

_____

_____

_____

_____

✽ WRITE IT DOWN

Describe a situation where someone spoke words of healing and life to you. How did you feel? Did those words make a lasting difference in your life? Describe a situation where you found it difficult to control your tongue, but you did. Do you think your self-control made a difference? Why?

Week 49
Married Love

✿ You Are a Garden

The Song of Solomon is a descriptive story about the love between a man and a woman. Solomon says to his future bride, "You are a garden locked up, my sister, my bride; you are a spring enclosed, a sealed fountain" (Song of Songs 4:12). He found her especially beautiful because no one else had trespassed in her garden. It had been saved for him to enjoy. He delighted in her love.

Love and sex are supposed to be delightful. God wants us to find that one person about whom we can say, "My lover is mine and I am his" (Song of Songs 2:16). That person is to know you as no one else knows you. My precious husband, Stu, knows my deepest secrets. He not only knows what makes me laugh and cry, but he has seen and done things with me that no one else has. It's a bond that is right. Don't spoil the intimacy you are to have with your husband alone by sharing it with someone else.

In a time of weakness, it can be easy to spoil the beautiful relationship God has prepared for you. You are so special and so unique. Don't give away what God created just for you and your future husband to enjoy.

GET INTO THE WORD

1. Read 1 Corinthians 7:2–4 and fill in the blanks. *Each man should have his own _____, and each woman her own _____. The husband should fulfill his _____ duty to his wife, and likewise the wife to her husband. The wife's _____ does not belong to her alone but _____ to her husband. In the same way, the husband's body does not _____ to him alone but also to his wife.*

2. Why do you think it is so important for sex to be confined only to marriage? _____

   _____

   _____

   _____

   _____

3. Do you think marriage changes love? In what ways? _____

   _____

   _____

   _____

   _____

❋ HEAR GOD'S VOICE

Give honor to marriage, and remain faithful to one another in marriage.

—Hebrews 13:4 NLT

❋ LIVE IT OUT

This week I will renew my commitment to share my body only with my future husband by _____

_____

_____

_____

_____

_____

_____

_____

❉ WRITE IT DOWN

What do you think are the primary benefits of waiting for married love?
Can you think of any other aspects of married love besides sex? What
are they? Write a letter to your future husband, telling him why you are
waiting for him.

Week 50
Journaling

❀ THOUGHTS AND DREAMS

I have been journaling since I was in junior high, except back then I called it writing in my diary. There is something very freeing about writing your thoughts to God. When I journal, I tell God my thoughts and dreams and fears and successes. Oh, I know that He already knows these things, but it has always been good for me to write them out. Some days I may write one sentence, and on other days I may take up several pages, writing from the very depths of my soul.

Reading back through my journal, I am amazed at how much I've changed through the years. My life has been a bit of a roller coaster, and most of those ups and downs are written in the pages of my journals. The thing that leaves me awestruck is that the one thing that has never changed in all my years of journal entries is the presence of God. He was and is always there, and as I read through the pages of my life, I am so encouraged to see His faithfulness.

Today, I want to encourage you to begin journaling. I promise that when you look back years later, you, too, will be amazed at how actively involved God is in your life.

GET INTO THE WORD

1. When you write down your thoughts, you give them substance and permanence. Do you think this statement is true? Why or why not? _____

   _____

   _____

   _____

2. What are some of the benefits of journaling mentioned on page 200? _____

   _____

   _____

   _____

3. How can journaling bring us closer to the Lord? _____

   _____

   _____

   _____

4. What tools will you need to begin journaling? _____

   _____

   _____

   _____

I'm thanking you, God, from a full heart,
I'm writing the book on your wonders.

—*Psalm 9:1* MSG

🌸 LIVE IT OUT

This week I will begin the habit of journaling my thoughts to God by gathering the tools I need (a notebook, journal, or diary and a special pen) and choosing a certain time each day to write.

_____

_____

_____

_____

_____

❀ WRITE IT DOWN

Practice your new journaling habit by writing your thoughts to God.
Pour out your heart to Him. Tell Him how much it means to you to be
His child. Write Him a poem or a song that comes straight from your
heart.

_____

_____

_____

_____

_____

_____

_____

_____

_____

_____

_____

Week 51
God's Forgiveness

❀ His Own Little Boy

I have known of God's love ever since I was a toddler in the nursery at church. But this past year, I saw God's love in a new way—our son, Spence, was born. As I held our son in my arms for the first time, I got an idea of how much God must love us. Stu and I gazed at Spence in amazement; we counted every finger and toe. His hands looked just like his daddy's, and his mouth was just like mine.

As his mother, I knew I would do anything to protect him—I couldn't imagine how I would feel if something happened to that little boy. That's when it hit me. God must have loved His own little boy even more than I love mine. Yet, He allowed His only Son to walk upon this cruel earth, knowing that He would have to suffer excruciating pain and die on a cross. God did that for you and me.

If God loved us that much, don't you think He was already prepared to forgive us? No matter what you've done, God is willing and able to forgive you, my friend. Just ask Him.

GET INTO THE WORD

1. Read Psalm 86:5 (NCV) and fill in the blanks. *Lord, you are*
   _____ *and* _____ *and have great love for* _____
   who call to _____.

2. How are forgiveness and love intertwined? _____
   _____
   _____
   _____
   _____
   _____

3. How many times will God forgive us when we ask with a truly
   repentant heart? Explain your answer. _____
   _____
   _____
   _____
   _____
   _____
   _____

Hear God's Voice

Blessed are those whose iniquities
are forgiven,
and whose sins are covered.
Blessed is the one against whom the Lord
will not reckon sin.

—*Romans 4:7–8* NRSV

Live It Out

This week I will seek God's forgiveness by ______________________

WRITE IT DOWN

Describe a time when you felt God's forgiveness pour over your heart. How did it feel? Write a letter to God telling Him how much His forgiveness means to you and how it has changed your life.

God's Love

🌸 More Than Anything

How can we come to understand God's love for us? First and foremost, we must remember what He did for each individual person—that means me and you—by allowing His Son to die on the cross. The Bible tells us that we are sinners and that the wages of sin is death. In this case, death means the presence of hell and the absence of heaven, for all eternity. But God, because of His love for us, didn't want us to endure what we deserve, so He sent His only Son to die as a sacrifice for me and for you. That God would do this for us proves beyond a shadow of a doubt that He really does love people more than anything.

"More than anything"—that means that to God, nothing comes before us. My own priorities often get way out of whack, but God's never do. In every circumstance, no matter what we are going through, we can be assured that God loves us more than anything.

I have found that when I ask God to comfort me with the assurance of His love, He faithfully honors that request. In God's love is where you find self-worth and confidence, not to mention the most significant love of your life.

Get into the Word

1. Read Psalm 33:18 and fill in the blanks. *The _____ of the LORD are on those who _____ him, on those whose _____ is in his _____ love.*

2. Why do you think God loves you so completely? _____

   _____

   _____

   _____

3. According to page 208, what two important things do we find in God's love? _____

   _____

   _____

   _____

   _____

4. How does God's love compare to the other loves in your life? ___

   _____

   _____

   _____

   _____

✾ HEAR GOD'S VOICE

Blessed be the LORD,
    for he has wondrously shown
        his steadfast love to me.

                    —*Psalm 31:21 NRSV*

✾ LIVE IT OUT

This week I will share God's love with someone I know by _____

_____

_____

_____

_____

_____

_____

❋ WRITE IT DOWN

Describe how it makes you feel to know you are loved by God. Write Him a love letter letting Him know you love Him in return and why.

_____

_____

_____

_____

_____

_____

_____

_____

_____

_____

_____

_____

_____

_____

_____

_____

ANSWERS TO FILL-IN-THE-BLANK QUESTIONS

Week 1 May the God of hope fill you with all joy and peace as you trust in him, so that you may overflow with hope by the power of the Holy Spirit. —Romans 15:13

Week 2 Obey your leaders and submit to their authority. They keep watch over you as men who must give an account. Obey them so that their work will be a joy, not a burden, for that would be of no advantage to you. —Hebrews 13:17

Week 3 How can a young person live a pure life? He can do it by obeying your word. With all my heart I try to obey you, God. Don't let me break your commands. I have taken your words to heart so I would not sin against you. —Psalm 119:9–11

Week 4 Everything that was written in the past was written to teach us, so that through endurance and the encouragement of the Scriptures we might have hope. —Romans 15:4

Week 5 No discipline seems pleasant at the time, but painful. Later on, however, it produces a harvest of righteousness and peace for those who have been trained by it. —Hebrews 12:11

Week 6 Praise be to the God and Father of our Lord Jesus Christ, who has blessed us in the heavenly realms with every spiritual blessing in Christ. For he chose us in him before the creation of the world to be holy and blameless in his sight. In love he predestined us to be adopted as his sons through Jesus Christ, in accordance with his pleasure and will. —Ephesians 1:3–6

Week 7 Praise be to the God and Father of our Lord Jesus Christ, the Father of compassion and the God of all comfort, who comforts us in all our troubles, so that we can comfort those in any trouble with the comfort we ourselves have received from God. —2 Corinthians 1:3–4

Week 8 I am convinced that neither death nor life, neither angels nor demons, neither the present nor the future, nor any powers, neither height nor depth, nor anything else in all creation, will be able to separate us from the love of God that is in Christ Jesus our Lord. —Romans 8:38–39

Week 9 When the kindness and love of God our Savior appeared, he saved us, not because of righteous things we had done, but because of his mercy. He saved us through the washing of rebirth and renewal by the Holy Spirit. —Titus 3:4–5

Week 10 You are the light of the world. A city on a hill cannot be hidden. Neither do people light a lamp and put it under a bowl. Instead they put it on its stand and it gives light to everyone in the house. In the same way, let your light shine before men, that they may see your good deeds and praise your Father in heaven. —Matthew 5:14–16

Week 11 Just as each of us has one body with many members, and these members do not all have the same function, so in Christ we who are many form one body, and each member belongs to all the others. We have different gifts, according to the grace given us. —Romans 12:4–6

Week 12 Your compassion is great, O Lord; preserve my life according to your laws. —Psalm 119:156

Week 13 When your words came, I ate them; they were my joy and my heart's delight, for I bear your name, O Lord God Almighty. —Jeremiah 15:16

Week 14 Jesus said to her, "I am the resurrection and the life. He who believes in me will live, even though he dies; and whoever lives and believes in me will never die. Do you believe this?" —John 11:25–26

Week 15 "I know the plans I have for you," declares the Lord, "plans to prosper you and not to harm you, plans to give you hope and a future." —Jeremiah 29:11

Week 16 Everyone must submit himself to the governing authorities, for there is no authority except that which God has established. The authorities that exist have been established by God. —Romans 13:1

Week 17 Your word is a lamp to my feet and a light for my path. —Psalm 119:105

Week 18 Be devoted to one another in brotherly love. Honor one another above yourselves. —Romans 12:10

Week 19 The Lord does not look at the things man looks at. Man looks at the outward appearance, but the Lord looks at the heart. —1 Samuel 16:7

Week 20 Jesus said, "Whoever has my commands and obeys them, he is the one who loves me. He who loves me will be loved by my Father, and I too will love him and show myself to him." —John 14:21

Week 21 Love is patient, love is kind. It does not boast, it is not proud. It is not rude, it is not self-seeking, it is not easily angered, it keeps no record of wrongs.

Love does not delight in evil but rejoices with the truth. It always protects, always trusts, always hopes, always perseveres. Love never fails. —1 Corinthians 13:4–8

Week 22 [Jesus said]: "Greater love has no one than this, that he lay down his life for his friends. You are my friends if you do what I command." —John 15:13–14

Week 23 The Word of God is living and active. Sharper than any two-edged sword, it penetrates even to dividing soul and spirit, joints and marrow; it judges the thoughts and attitudes of the heart. —Hebrews 4:12

Week 24 As a father has compassion on his children, so the Lord has compassion on those who fear him. —Psalm 103:13

Week 25 Imitate those who through faith and patience inherit what has been promised. —Hebrews 6:12

Week 26 Do you not know that your body is a temple of the Holy Spirit, who is in you, whom you have received from God? You are not your own; you were bought at a price. Therefore honor God with your body. —1 Corinthians 6:19–20

Week 27 You have made known to me the path of life; you will fill me with joy in your presence, with eternal pleasures at your right hand. —Psalm 16:11

Week 28 As God's chosen people, holy and dearly loved, clothe yourselves with compassion, kindness, humility, gentleness and patience. Bear with each other and forgive whatever grievances you may have against one another. Forgive as the Lord forgave you. And over all these virtues put on love, which binds them all together in perfect unity. —Colossians 3:12–14

Week 29 Do not be anxious about anything, but in everything, by prayer and petition, with thanksgiving, present your requests to God. And the peace of God, which transcends all understanding, will guard your hearts and your minds in Christ Jesus. —Philippians 4:6–7

Week 30 Remind the people to be subject to rulers and authorities, to be obedient, to be ready to do whatever is good. —Titus 3:1

Week 31 The Lord says, "I will save the one who loves me. I will keep him safe, because he trusts in me. He will call out to me, and I will answer him. I will be with him in times of trouble. I will save him and honor him." —Psalm 91:14–15

Week 32 God our Savior . . . wants all people to be saved and he wants everyone to know the truth. There is only one God and there is only one way that people can reach God. That way is through Jesus Christ, who is also a man. —1 Timothy 2:3–5

Week 33 When you're unmarried, you're free to concentrate on simply pleasing the Master. . . . All I want is for you to be able to develop a way of life in which you can spend plenty of time together with the Master without a lot of distractions. —1 Corinthians 7:32

Week 34 We do not have a high priest who is unable to sympathize with our weaknesses, but we have one who has been tempted in every way, just as we are—yet without sin. Let us then approach the throne of grace with confidence, so that we may receive mercy and find grace to help us in our time of need. —Hebrews 4:15–16

Week 35 [The Lord] holds victory in store for the upright, he is a shield to those whose walk is blameless, for he guards the course of the just and protects the way of his faithful ones. —Proverbs 2:7–8

Week 36 We know that God causes everything to work together for the good of those who love God and are called according to his purpose for them. —Romans 8:28

Week 37 Do not offer the parts of your body to sin, as instruments of wickedness, but rather offer yourselves to God, as those who have been brought from death to life; and offer the parts of your body to him as instruments of righteousness. —Romans 6:13

Week 38 The man who looks intently into the perfect law that gives freedom, and continues to do this, not forgetting what he has heard, but doing it—he will be blessed in what he does. —James 1:25

Week 39 You created my inmost being; you knit me together in my mother's womb. I praise you because I am fearfully and wonderfully made; your works are wonderful, I know that full well. —Psalm 139:13–14

Week 40 The fruit of righteousness will be peace; the effect of righteousness will be quietness and confidence forever. My people will live in peaceful dwelling places, in secure homes, in undisturbed places of rest. —Isaiah 32:17–18

Week 41 Each one should use whatever gift he has received to serve others, faithfully administering God's grace in its various forms. If anyone speaks, he should do it as one speaking the very words of God. If anyone serves, he should do it with the strength God provides, so that in all things God may be praised through Jesus Christ. —1 Peter 4:10–11

Week 42 [God, our Savior] saved us, not because of righteous things we had done, but because of his mercy. He saved us through the washing of rebirth and renewal by the Holy Spirit, whom he poured out on us generously through Jesus Christ our Savior, so that, having been justified by his grace, we might become heirs having the hope of eternal life. —Titus 3:5–7

Week 43 Blessed is the man who perseveres under trial, because when he has stood the test, he will receive the crown of life that God has promised to those who love him. —James 1:12

Week 44 I have sought your face with all my heart; be gracious to me according to your promise. I have considered my ways and have turned my steps to your statutes. —Psalm 119:58–59

Week 45 Let us draw near to God with a sincere heart in full assurance of faith, having our hearts sprinkled to cleanse us from a guilty conscience and having our bodies washed with pure water. —Hebrews 10:22

Week 46 The Lord is close to the brokenhearted and saves those who are crushed in spirit. —Psalm 34:18

Week 47 Be strong in the Lord and in his mighty power. Put on the full armor of God so that you can take your stand against the devil's schemes. For our struggle is not against flesh and blood, but against the rulers, against the authorities, against the powers of this dark world and against the spiritual forces of evil in the heavenly realms. —Ephesians 6:10–12

Week 48 Reckless words pierce like a sword, but the tongue of the wise brings healing. —Proverbs 12:18

Week 49 Each man should have his own wife, and each woman her own husband. The husband should fulfill his marital duty to his wife, and likewise the wife to her husband. The wife's body does not belong to her alone but also to her husband. In the same way, the husband's body does not belong to him alone but also to his wife. —1 Corinthians 7:2–4

Week 50 (No fill-in-the-blank)

Week 51 Lord, you are kind and forgiving and have great love for those who call to you. —Psalm 86:5

Week 52 The eyes of the Lord are on those who fear him, on those whose hope is in his unfailing love. —Psalm 33:18

TOPICAL INDEX

Acceptance	26	Life	126
Assurance	34	Loving God	82
Authority	66	Loving Others	86
Bible Reading	154	Marriage	134
Comfort	30	Married Love	198
Compassion	98	Obedience	122
Dating	150	Parents	10
Differences	46	Patience	102
Discipline	22	Prayer	118
Divorce	186	Purity	14
Encouragement	18	Quiet Time	178
Eternal Life	58	Boy Decisions	78
Family	74	Rules	50
Friendship with God	90	Salvation	38
God's Faithfulness	70	Scripture Memorization	54
God's Forgiveness	206	Self-image	158
God's Grace	170	Sex	106
God's Love	210	Suffering	174
God's Mercy	138	Talent and Gifts	166
God's Peace	162	Temptation	190
God's Presence	110	Trusting God	6
God's Promises	146	Truth	130
God's Word	94	Unity	114
Guilt	182	Victory	142
Hope	62	Witnessing	42
Journaling	202	Words	194

REFERENCES

About the Authors

Point of Grace: For fifteen years, Point of Grace has built a successful career delivering songs of substance. Through the Girls of Grace conferences, Shelley Breen, Leigh Cappillino, Denise Jones, and Heather Payne have used their unique gifts to inspire teenage girls to lead pure, godly lives. Point of Grace has sold more than five million albums, netted eight Dove Awards, and received two Grammy nods. They've been awarded two Platinum and five Gold albums and have scored an impressive twenty-four #1 singles on Christian radio. Over the years, they've toured relentlessly and through the Girls of Grace conferences have educated, ministered to, and encouraged more than one hundred thousand young women throughout the past five years.